King Solomon and Ashmedai: A Wisdom Tale

by

Barak A. Bassman

Cover designed by Telemachus Press, LLC

Cover art:
Copyright © iStock/187481052/duncan1890

Published by Telemachus Press, LLC
http://www.telemachuspress.com

Library of Congress Control Number: 2017932066

ISBN: 978-1-945330-39-1 (eBook)
ISBN: 978-1-945330-40-7 (Paperback)
ISBN: 978-1-945330-41-4 (Hardback)

FICTION / Mythology see Fairy Tales, Folk Tales, Legends & Mythology

Version 2017.01.28

King Solomon and Ashmedai: A Wisdom Tale

I. The Capture of the Devil

WORD REACHED KING Solomon that Ashmedai had been captured. Now, flanked by two soldiers and Solomon's swaggering aide-de-camp Benaiah, and shackled in golden fetters engraved with secret and potent names of the Holy One, the king of the demons entered the throne room where the king of Israel was holding court. Tall and muscular, with black hair falling in smooth waves over his chest, Ashmedai did not writhe under his chains, or try to free himself, but stood straight with his broad shoulders thrown back, smirking contemptuously at young King Solomon.

Solomon looked away from the prisoner and across the crowded room. Unnerved by the intense stares of the onlookers, he turned back towards Ashmedai. The demon king's arrogant grin had grown wider, and he had tilted his head coquettishly to one side so that his black wavy locks slid down his upper arm. Knowing he was expected to act boldly, Solomon glared into Ashmedai's eyes and scolded him:

Foul demon king, you are now a prisoner of the Kingdom of Israel. The Holy One, Blessed be He, has delivered you unto me. Now tell me where I can find the *shamir.*

Solomon's voice cracked on the word *shamir.*

The *shamir* was the reason for capturing Ashmedai. Solomon had decided to resurrect his father King David's aborted idea of building a Temple in Jerusalem, which would be a dwelling place for the Holy One, Blessed be He, and for the sacred Ark of the Covenant. There was a difficulty, however. The Temple would need to be built, in large part, of stone, and the stone pieces would need to be cut and molded into the proper shapes. Solomon's builders naturally suggested iron tools to cut and fashion the stone blocks, until the prophets and soothsayers at the king's court protested that the Holy One, Blessed be He, had forbidden the use of iron tools in the building of His dwelling place, as these were instruments of war and discord.

Solomon asked how the builders were supposed to cut the stones.

With the *shamir*, the soothsayers answered. The *shamir* was a giant worm that had once lived in the Garden of Eden and could cut through rock.

Where is the *shamir*? asked Solomon.

We do not know, answered the soothsayers. But Ashmedai, king of the demons, can locate the *shamir* for you. Capture Ashmedai.

This is madness, Solomon told himself. How could he capture the king of the demons? His building program would collapse amidst the snickering whispers of backbiting courtiers. But he swore he could not let that happen.

Acting on the king's detailed instructions, the royal smiths fashioned a set of gold fetters engraved with a series of unmentionable esoteric true names for the Holy One, Blessed be He, which had been revealed to Solomon in his dreams. The king then summoned his soothsayers and ordered them to conjure a demon; his soldiers caught him in the enchanted gold chains. The scaly, writhing imp tore futilely at his bonds until he finally revealed the mountaintop where Ashmedai rested in the afternoons and drank water from an underground spring.

Solomon devised a trap for the king of the demons, dispatching Benaiah with a cohort of soldiers and a barrel of strong wine, which Benaiah, following the king's instructions, carefully emptied into the interior hollow of the boulder from which Ashmedai drank. As dusk fell, a broadly built man with beautiful black hair came down from the sky, landing leisurely with a soft thud by a seal on the rock. After absent-mindedly mumbling an incantation to roll the stone open, the hulking man took a small pitcher out of his satchel and scooped up the wine to his lips without looking at it. A moment later Ashmedai staggered and fell unconscious from the strong drink. Benaiah seized the opportunity to throw the same set of enchanted golden chains upon the drunken king of the demons.

And now it was time to reap the benefit of all this plotting and trapping: the demon king would reveal the location of the *shamir*. But Ashmedai merely arched his eyebrows and asked what use His Majesty had for the *shamir*. Surely a great monarch, heir to the conquering King David, already had his choice of the finest worms in the kingdom?

You know why.

Leaning forward on his throne, Solomon had raised his voice without realizing it.

We need the *shamir* to build the Temple, the dwelling place for the Holy One, Blessed be He, and the Ark of His Covenant. Now where is it?

After heaving a theatrical sigh, Ashmedai replied slowly:

Your Majesty, great and mighty King Solomon, I do not understand all this fuss over a silly little worm. But, regardless, I am no help to you in your eccentric quest. I do not keep the *shamir*. I gave him, as a gift, to the Leviathan, lord of the sea. Your esteemed Majesty wasted all that fine wine for no good reason, alas.

Solomon fell back in his throne, as he felt his exuberance slip away down some deep hole—Why was building this temple so difficult? There were temples everywhere to so many gods—why was it so hard for him to build one structure for one deity?

A tear of self-pity fell down his cheek. Quickly wiping it away, Solomon composed himself, silently cursing his tear ducts and turning back to Ashmedai:

You will not be released from your chains until you are of some help. What did the Leviathan do with the *shamir*? Must we dredge the seas now?

The crowd in the room was silent. Benaiah stared down at his feet and sighed, while Solomon's leg shook violently.

After letting the silence linger uncomfortably for several minutes, Ashmedai finally spoke:

The Leviathan had no use for the *shamir*. What good is a worm on the ocean floor? So the Leviathan gave him as a gift to the great eagle, king of the birds, who makes his nest atop Mount Tabor. You should ask the eagle to lend you the worm.

Trying to hide his frustration, Solomon turned his eyes to the ceiling. On one of the rotting old wooden beams, for some odd reason, sat an empty dust-coated glass jar, at which the king stared for some time, ignoring his prisoner and the assembled dignitaries.

King of the demons, Solomon said slyly, our audience is at an end. Benaiah, have the prisoner put in an empty room in the basement of the palace. Lock the room and keep guards posted. Come see me in my private rooms.

Three days later Benaiah and his soldiers marched again into the throne room. Once more, Solomon mounted his throne with innumerable jewels dangling from his fingers. The various royal courtiers dutifully filed in and packed the royal audience chamber.

Benaiah stood behind two soldiers, who were carrying a rectangular wooden box between them, and triumphantly rubbed his hands together. Solomon slouched lazily in his throne as he stared at an emerald ring on his left forefinger. Without looking up he asked Benaiah what was in the box.

In a raised voice, with his chest pushed forward, Benaiah announced: Your Majesty, we present to you the *shamir.*

King Solomon, of course, already knew the *shamir* was sitting—or wiggling?—in the box. He had sent Benaiah off with instructions to find the eagle's nest on the high mountaintop, where Benaiah was to place a large glass jar over the eagle's chicks. As Solomon had predicted, once the eagle saw the jar imprisoning its young, it fetched the *shamir* to break it.

When Benaiah saw the *shamir* dropped from the eagle's claws onto the glass jar he pounced upon it with a large sack and captured the magical worm.

King Solomon instructed Benaiah to open the box—and there it was: the *shamir*, an unusually large worm, about the length of a grown man's arm, with slimy grey skin and two tiny eyes, almost like dots etched onto its flesh. Yet the worm's most striking feature was its mouth, which was packed with several dense rows of razor sharp teeth.

Can it cut stones? King Solomon asked.

Benaiah tossed a small stone from his pocket in front of the *shamir*, which promptly sliced it clean in half. King Solomon swooned with self-satisfaction: He had outfoxed the demon king and the great eagle, and he was going to build the Temple in Jerusalem as a dwelling place for the Holy One, Blessed be He. Forever after, all the people of Israel would travel to see it and offer sacrifices there, in awe of King Solomon's immortal achievement.

The courtiers were now cheering and speaking excitedly as the bright, warm sun filtered in through the slits in the windows. Even the *shamir* seemed to catch the current of glee it had unleashed, giddily bobbing its head up and down as it cut the stone into ever finer slices.

Amidst the rejoicing, Solomon recalled he had Ashmedai still locked up in the palace basement. Should the demon king be released now? He had the *shamir*, which had been the point of capturing Ashmedai—and it was not as if the Israelites needed a demon to help build a sacred temple. The king reflected on his promise—well, not exactly a promise, but arguably implied—he would release Ashmedai if the demon king helped to secure the *shamir*. And the king of the demons had proved, somewhat contrary to his reputation, to be a creature of his word. So, Solomon told himself, you should release Ashmedai.

But if he released him, would Ashmedai not seek vengeance against Solomon for trapping and humiliating him—if for no other reason than to maintain his dignity before his demon subjects? Would the demon king stir up Solomon's enemies in Jerusalem? Or maybe foment wars on Solomon's borders? Ashmedai had powers far beyond those of a mortal man, so Solomon could not be sure of what he was, and was not, capable (or willing). No, better to keep him locked up. A demon on the loose would not do anything but wreak chaos and destruction.

And one cannot be certain of the future, Solomon mused, so perhaps I may need Ashmedai's occult powers someday. What if I should discover I am in need of another magic creature? Ashmedai will not let himself be caught again—the demon king's guard will be up now. Yes, Ashmedai may be needed at some point in the future, so it would be prudent to keep him in his room, locked and guarded.

Thus, as the impromptu celebration in the throne room raged around him, King Solomon, ignoring it all, had come to the firm decision to continue hosting the king of demons indefinitely in his royal palace in Jerusalem.

II. The Devil Offers Sage Counsel

WITH THE *SHAMIR* in hand, work on building the Temple finally commenced. The site was picked within Jerusalem, on a largely empty lot (the few squatters were discretely escorted away). The *shamir* and its new keeper came each morning to the building site to cut stones imported from various quarries. The going was slow—one worm, no matter how magical, could only cut through so much stone at a time—but the *shamir* made steady progress.

The trouble was the next step: taking the stone pieces, and the wood and gold to be used for the interior, and actually building the Temple. King Solomon soon realized there was a lack of available manpower. The soldiers were needed to keep order and maintain the security of the borders. The royal household had only a small staff, as King David had not seen the need for them, and what staff there was consisted of round, soft-bellied men who excelled in cooking and managing the wine cellars, but did not seem capable of hauling stones.

Solomon considered hiring laborers. But with King David's conquests, the Israelites had expanded their land faster than their population, so that each family could barely muster the labor to work its own fields and care for its own flocks. Nor did he wish to import foreign workers: not only would he need to find some way to house, clothe, and feed them all, but he was terrified of the wrath of the Holy One, Blessed be He, should idolaters clutching little statues of their false gods wander the grounds of the Temple, His home and dwelling place in His holy, promised land. So the stones continued to pile up on the building site, which shifted from a source of pride into a conspicuous display of impotence.

Solomon's leading courtiers requested a meeting with him, privately, at night. Six burly men, barely contained within their coarse white linen robes, filed into the king's bedchamber shortly before midnight. The king of Israel faced them sitting upright against his bedpost in his blue-striped silk nightgown, which hung loosely on his gangly frame.

The men stood in a semi-circle around the young king's bed. Looking at the group in the dim candlelight, he thought they appeared like monsters risen from a terrifying underworld, who intended to tear him to pieces with their hairy, callused hands. Remember the would-be kingships of Adonijah and Absalom, my felled, usurper brothers, Solomon thought. Kings can get their pretty, long locks caught in tree branches and find themselves cut down like wild game. Kingship can be a fragile affair.

Benaiah, the spokesman of the group, bowed his head, and addressed his king:

Your Majesty, thank you for granting us this audience. You know we served your father, the mighty King David, loyally for many years. When David's days were at their end, we recognized you as his true heir and were not seduced by your brother Adonijah's lies and usurpations. I killed Adonijah myself with these hands and this sword, just as the foul traitor deserved.

Your Majesty, we are worried. Evil tongues are slandering you across Jerusalem, and even in the countryside. The *shamir* cuts stones, but then the stones sit on a heap in the sun. Some say—and I only repeat these words so Your Majesty can appreciate the depth of the wickedness of some men in this city—some say the king is a fickle youth, who has lost interest in building the Temple for the Holy One, Blessed be He. These evil men make jokes about how Your Majesty is like a small child who claps at his dancing pet worm, but does nothing serious.

There are worse men yet. Abiathar, the priest, you may recall, supported your brother Adonijah's unlawful usurpation of your throne. You exiled him. I counseled you to kill him, but Your Majesty, in your great mercy, recognized Abiathar's loyal years of service to the Holy One, Blessed be He, and to King David, and spared him. Now Abiathar sends whispers from abroad to his old priestly colleagues that you have abandoned building the Temple because you no longer fear and follow the Holy One, Blessed be He, the lord of this land who brought us forth from the house of bondage, the land of Egypt, with a mighty hand and an outstretched arm. Abiathar hints that you have been seduced by foreign gods, or perhaps even Ashmedai himself, and that the wrath of the Holy One,

Blessed be He, will be terrible. Israel, Abiathar says, will be punished severely for King Solomon's sins.

Your Majesty, we beg you, find a way to begin work on the Temple, even just a little. Move some stones. It will allow the many good men who surround you to silence the vicious slanderers and to drive away the remnant of Adonijah's cause.

Solomon's advisors now seemed less like monsters and more like scared children. The king grasped how they feared his fall from power, as they and their families would be cut down by the new king as Solomon had once butchered so many of Adonijah's supporters. Feeling a surge of power—those gnarled hairy hands were bound to him—Solomon nevertheless understood he needed to provide reassurance:

Benaiah, and my dear friends, have you not learned to have faith in my wisdom? I outwit the king of the demons and the great eagle, king of the birds. Do you think my wisdom will fail against a senile priest and a smattering of jokesters? You will see, soon, the Temple will be built. It is late. Go home, rest yourselves.

The burly men bowed and slowly filed out the door. He could not tell if his bluff had worked, as he had, in truth, no idea how to marshal the manpower to build the Temple. Despite the late hour, sleep would not return to the worried king of Israel, who found himself restlessly pacing his room.

Eventually, Solomon summoned the guards posted outside his suite of apartments. To the palace basement, he instructed them. The basement was a long, narrow corridor with rooms opening on each side. The walls were spare, and smudged with soot and ash. The area had been used by the original merchant owner of the building for storing grain, wine, and honey.

Solomon, however, was now storing Ashmedai there, whom he had, by and large, ignored since learning the whereabouts of the *shamir.* But now it seemed prudent to seek Ashmedai's counsel. The king of the demons was, after all, as old as creation and knew many secrets. Perhaps he had a solution to the labor shortage or could recall a similar problem from ages past. Solomon briefly marveled that Ashmedai had made no attempt to escape, or had his demon subjects attempt a rescue (or even any retaliation), but Solomon chalked this up to the favor and blessing of the Holy One, Blessed be He, to the pious king of Israel.

The demon king's cell was halfway down the corridor, flanked by guards playing with a pair of dice on the floor. Startled by the loud announcement of their upstairs colleague that His Majesty was demanding an immediate audience with the prisoner, the men fumbled clumsily to reassemble their gear.

Solomon ignored them and, taking a torch from one of the guards, entered the prisoner's cell. Ashmedai was sprawled on his back, looking up at the ceiling and singing some tune softly in a language Solomon did not know. The demon king's lush raven hair and closely trimmed beard looked freshly washed and smelled of a floral perfume, even though none of this seemed possible in the prison cell. Indifferent to the drafty air in the damp basement room, his naked muscular body gleamed invitingly in the torchlight. Solomon, feeling small and weak, had a sudden urge to bury his narrow bony frame in that broad chest and to sniff the sweetly fragrant black hair.

Ashmedai stopped singing, but did not look at his visitor. Can I be of assistance to His Majesty? he asked.

Solomon willed himself to speak sternly.

Quiet, demon. I would be glad to let you sit here and rot for eternity, but it occurs to me that nothing happens without a reason, and the Holy One, Blessed be He, must have delivered you into my hands and kept you here for a purpose. So I will see if I can make use of you.

Ashmedai made no response. Feeling uncomfortable in the silence, Solomon spoke further, if only to reassure himself:

We captured the *shamir*, and it has sliced many stones at my command.

Ashmedai closed his eyes and picked up his song.

Quiet demon!

As you wish, great king. My apologies for interrupting you. You were boasting of your wide dominion over worms and rocks?

Solomon felt a rush of hatred. Who was this insolent creature to laugh at him? The mightiest demon and he was ensnared by the brilliant king's superior wisdom. Nevertheless, he reminded himself he had come to this cell for a purpose, and could not let the demon king distract him from his holy and righteous endeavor.

Demon, I came here to discover whether you had any useful counsel to provide after all the ages you have wandered the Earth. Perhaps you are good for nothing more than finding worms. But I owe it to my people to try to make some use of my illustrious prisoner. I have accumulated a large pile of cut stones, but I have no laborers to take them and build the Temple, the dwelling place for the Holy One, Blessed be He. I have come to see if you have any suggestions as to how I can find the labor I need.

Ashmedai continued staring at the ceiling. After a pause, he laughed and offered his counsel:

You Israelites, always so inward-looking. Do you think you are the first king ever to build something? The answer is easy—import foreign slaves and set them to work.

But I cannot do that. They will bring idols of foreign gods into the work site and pray to them. The house of the Holy One, Blessed be He, will be defiled.

Well, then, wise and exalted majesty, the answer is still easy. If only Israelites can be trusted not to defile the site, use Israelites.

But there are not enough Israelite men.

Nonsense, Your Majesty. Here is what you should do: order each tribe of Israel to send its men to you one month out of the year to do whatever labor the crown needs. All the tribes' men. That will be enough workers, and it is only a month, so they can quickly return to their fields or goat flocks or whatnot.

Solomon considered this idea. Perhaps it would work, he thought. But then a new concern arose in the king's mind:

How could I pay for so much labor? The treasury will be empty if I have to hire so many Israelite workers. And there will be anger at the loss of available hands in each household.

Ashmedai rolled onto his side and looked at the king:

Your Majesty does not act like the earthly kings I have seen. Why pay them? Israel owes its kingdom and wealth to His blessing, so it is only fitting that, in gratitude, the Israelites give themselves freely to the task of building His temple. You are a selfish and ungrateful nation.

Solomon snapped back immediately:

But if the men are not paid, then they are slaves. The Holy One, Blessed be He, brought us forth from the house of bondage into freedom. He freed us from slavery in Egypt. His dwelling place cannot be a monument to slave labor.

Ashmedai rolled over onto his back again, and, running his fingers gently, almost flirtatiously, through his thick mane of hair, sighed dramatically.

Your Majesty is free to ignore my counsel, no matter how long my experience. It is, after all, Your Majesty, not I, who is famous for his great wisdom.

Solomon left the demon king without further word, hearing Ashmedai's soft singing once more as he walked away. Yet sleep still evaded him, leading him to pace furiously back and forth across his bed chamber as the sunrise penetrated the windows. The blood-red early morning light appeared menacing, as if the Holy One, Blessed be He, were rising in wrath at Solomon's failure to build the promised temple in Jerusalem. Considering his options again, he despaired of his situation, but finally concluded he must somehow move forward and came to a decision.

At the king of Israel's instruction, the scribe Elihoreph prepared twelve copies of a royal decree to go to the elders of each of the tribes of Israel: Each tribe, except the priestly tribe of Levi, was commanded to provide a fixed quota of men each month on a rotating basis to build the Temple. There would be no payment for this labor except the blessing of the Holy One, Blessed be He, who had brought them forth from slavery in Egypt and made them into a great nation and a mighty kingdom. Detachments of soldiers fanned out across the countryside to deliver these missives.

Within a week those tribal elders were in front of King Solomon in his throne room in Jerusalem, twelve old men with bald or balding heads and patchy grey beards. The elder of the tribe of Ephraim, Nebat, spoke on their behalf:

Your Majesty, we humbly thank you for receiving us. We traveled here as soon as we received the new royal decree. We are all in support of the pious project to build a Temple, a home, for the Holy One, Blessed be He, to crown His majesty in His people's kingdom. But your decree has made your people worry. Families do not want to lose their sons' labor for a month, especially with no pay. Is there no other way? Were we not freed from bondage in Egypt so we could be free men in our own promised land? We will all pay our fair share, but could we not raise funds for the purchase of foreign slaves, perhaps, who could do the work?

King Solomon leaned forward, decked out in full regalia—red silk robes, jewel-studded crown, rings on each finger—and with his tight brown curls soaked in perfumed oils, which smelled of overripe fruit. Benaiah stood by his side, armed with a spear and dressed for war. Soldiers were posted throughout the room. With relish, the king sprung his well-prepared rejoinder to the elders' arguments, which he had successfully anticipated in his great wisdom:

Distinguished elders, you know I always appreciate your counsel. Although I am sovereign, and although we will disagree at times, remember that you are always welcome here to share your views and to make sure the crown never loses sight of what the people of Israel feel. But as a king, I must sometimes make difficult decisions. I have sworn an oath to erect a Temple, a mighty dwelling place, for the Holy One, Blessed be He. He has seen how the idol worshippers around us raise imposing temples to their gods, even though their gods never delivered their people from bondage to Pharaoh, or gave them the conquering sword of King David, may his memory be blessed. Yet how does Israel show its gratitude to the Holy One, Blessed be He, for the wondrous miracles He has performed for our sake? We keep His Holy Ark, with His sacred words carved in stone, in ramshackle, makeshift shrines in the countryside. Where is His dwelling place in His people's promised land?

Early in my reign I had a dream vision of the Holy One, Blessed be He. He came to me in a great fiery cloud, like the pillar of fire that guided our forefathers when they wandered with our teacher, Moses, in the desert. He told me that, if I remained true to Him and forsook other gods, He would grant me whatever I wished. So I begged for the wisdom to know good from evil, and truth from falsehood, and the Holy One, Blessed be He, graced me with the wisdom I sought. With my new gift I could see how ungrateful Israel has been to our Lord and begged His forgiveness. I swore an oath, then and there, to build Him a Temple as His home in His people's land. Should I break that promise, I will bring His wrath upon us all.

But how to build such a Temple? First I needed the *shamir* to break the rocks. I outwitted Ashmedai, the demon king himself, to accomplish this feat. But now that I have cut the stones into pieces, I need men to move them. You

Israelites do not want to help. You want to bring in foreign slaves. Just imagine: On the site of His sacred Temple we will unleash a tidal wave of idolaters who deny Him, who will curse Him and call out to foreign gods, and litter the holy ground with their wretched little idols. His dwelling place will be defiled from the start. He will swell with rage and strike us down.

Your ancestors were slaves in Egypt who built temples for Pharaoh, the god king of the Egyptians, and for other Egyptian idols. But you will not lift a finger for your true Lord and God, the One who brought you forth from bondage? With such selfishness, such ingratitude from His people, do you think I can stave off His vengeance? We will surely fall again to our many enemies. We will be overrun and cut down.

King Solomon paused. The elders averted their eyes from him and from each other, making them appear stooped in shame. I bent their stiff necks with my words, he thought. Feeling smug, Solomon slouched back on his throne, and extended his right index finger, which dazzled with blue and green gemstones:

Nebat, elder of Ephraim, will you shirk from honoring the Holy One, Blessed be He, or will you show Him that His people love and appreciate Him?

Nebat answered weakly that the people of Israel would build His dwelling place in the holy city of Jerusalem. And as if those words were some secret signal, the tribal elders rapidly filed out of the throne room.

Thus began the construction of the holy Temple in Jerusalem. Each month a different tribe would send all of its able-bodied young men to the work site to follow the orders of Solomon's builders and architects. As the Israelites had no experience themselves in designing and erecting buildings, much less grand temples worthy of the Holy One, Blessed be He, Solomon had no choice but to hire architects and engineers from Egypt. The Israelites labored hard under these new Egyptian task masters, but feared to disobey. After all, His wrath could be terrible—no one wanted the kingdom to fall. Still, the curses floated up from under Israelite breaths and sometimes reached the Egyptians' ears. The Egyptians, with the approval of King Solomon, at times had to make an example of some particularly stubborn Israelite, whom they would whip until his back was crisscrossed by rivulets of blood.

King Solomon occasionally toured the work site. There were no more snickers and jabs, but instead eyes filled with hatred or fear. Good, he reflected, I can be loathed, that is fine for a king. But I cannot rule and be the butt of their jokes.

When the labor was completed, the Temple stood on a high hilltop in Jerusalem, visible for miles around. The exterior was made from the *shamir*'s finely cut stones. Inside were two rooms. The front room was spacious, with wooden walls decorated with etchings of gourds and flowers, an altar for sacrifices to the Holy One, Blessed be He, and benches for the Israelites to sit and pray. Behind this front room was a second, smaller room, the Holy of Holies, with floor, ceiling, and walls made of gold, just large enough to contain the Holy Ark of the Covenant and one man to beseech the Holy One, Blessed be He, to remember and look kindly upon His people Israel.

On the moonlit, warm night when the priests conveyed the Ark of the Covenant into the Temple's inner sanctum, Solomon entered the Holy of Holies with a torch in his hand, where he looked upon the Ark, but did not touch it because he well knew that to touch the Ark was to touch the Holy One himself, and that entailed certain death. Everything was quiet, as the gold in the Holy of Holies reflected brightly in the torchlight.

At that moment, King Solomon felt himself to be a far greater king than his father, the brutish, petty warlord. The Temple was a worthy rival to the monuments the Pharaohs had scattered across their cities and deserts. Like the mightiest pyramids, this Temple, the dwelling place for the Holy One, Blessed be He, would stand eternal and terrifying throughout all the generations to come, a permanent, immortal testimonial to the wisdom and power of the famous king who built it.

III. The Devil as Matchmaker

KING SOLOMON WAS in need of a queen, but it was not easy to find a bride. King David had been famously handsome—battle scarred in just the right amount to be rugged and not too pretty. David's sons were even more famously dashing, especially Adonijah, with his thick, luscious black hair falling below his shoulders and his taut, supple body. Adonijah's movements were confident and graceful, displaying the comfort around girls of a natural flirt. He would stealthily approach a palace lady, strolling amidst the hills of Jerusalem towards sunset, and drop an improvised crown of flowers onto the startled girl's head. But when she, indignant, turned around and saw Adonijah, her angry pout would melt away into blushes and stammers as she looked down, so he would not see how happy she was to be that night's anointed queen of the sunset.

It was different for Solomon. The boy was a runt: a flimsy noodle whose face, as a young man, was overrun by pimples, and whose hair was a mess of short, uneven curls.

He tried to make up for his lack of physical bulk with jewels and perfumes, some stolen from his mother's toilette. His mother, Queen Bathsheba, would chide him: this was no way for a boy to behave, especially the son of the world's most famous soldier. But Solomon felt reassured by the dense fog of sweet flowery scents and would not desist.

His first forays into the realm of love had not been successful. To begin with, there was the unfortunate affair of the Levite girl. She was slightly older, and petite, with soft red hair and a kind smile. They had met at a banquet celebrating some battle or other, which King David had won over some Philistine warlord or other on the Mediterranean coast—in his youth, Solomon never could keep these battles and warlords straight. The Levite girl was seated near Solomon's table. He had found himself ignored and alone at the celebration, as he had nothing to say about the battle.

The red-headed girl was also alone. Solomon stared at her, unable to tear his gaze away even though he knew he was being rude and should look elsewhere. Feeling acutely the young prince's uncomfortably intense glare, she came over to ask if he wanted anything from her, although she stood back at a respectful distance, arms rigid at her sides. Despite feeling suddenly overheated and disoriented, he eventually had the presence of mind to invite her to sit at his couch and keep him company. The girl obeyed, although she sat at the far end away from him, with her back ramrod straight and her hands tightly folded on her lap.

Not knowing what else to do, Solomon told her how he had been studying different languages, including the language of the just vanquished Philistines, which had all sorts of odd but fascinating grammatical quirks, which he proceeded to enumerate in detail. The girl nodded slightly. Taking this as encouragement, he launched into a lengthy disquisition on the similarities and differences between the Hebrew of the Israelites and the Greek of the coastal Philistines, comparing and contrasting different words and concepts between the two peoples and their languages. The girl's eyes grew steadily more vacant, which in turn prompted him to speak ever more fervently in an attempt to rouse them back to life.

Then he saw her eye slide to the side, as her line of sight snaked around Solomon to—he was sure of it—Adonijah, boasting in a corner, his cup raised high at a wild angle, spilling wine onto the floor. Solomon stopped talking. The girl apologized: She just now recalled she was supposed to help her mother at home with mending some old garments. Where had the time gone? She had departed before Solomon fully realized what she had said.

He tried to visit her in the following weeks, but his luck was poor: He always arrived right as she was leaving. Or when she was in the middle of some urgent chore. Or she was gone and would not be back for hours. Solomon would approach her house with his mind a riot of imaginary scenes in which the girl stroked his arm and gushed as he expounded on some piece of wisdom or other. Yet in the real, waking world he was perpetually rebuffed in the most courteous style—really, the girl said, she would love to talk, but unfortunately this happened to be a terrible time, she had sworn to bring these jars of honey before *Shabbat* to her grandmother—and each time he walked away, slowly, beating back tears—and the need to beat back his tears filled him with shame.

Solomon would drift away from the clogged, noisy streets of Jerusalem to a quiet hill where he could sit in solitude. On these hills the world seemed to be covered in a sticky film of sadness, which clung to his skin. He would look at the horizon, thinking of the girl's pretty, pale face, the one he wanted to gaze at so much, with longing and despair.

And then one night, as he sat on this sad lonely hill, there was that same red-headed Levite girl walking down below with several of her friends, and everyone was laughing. She jumped in front of the group to perform some kind of dance, although he could not make it out exactly. But then a tall muscular figure, barely contained in his flimsy cloak, stole up behind her to place a crown of freshly picked flowers upon her head, his long black hair tumbling over his shoulders onto her pale cheek. Spinning around with joyous squeals, her face lit up into a wide smile. In the pink light of the sunset, Solomon watched his brother, Adonijah, greedily kiss the girl for whom he had ached so often.

The situation with Abishag had only made things worse. When King David was old and ailing, his advisors thought he needed a beautiful young girl to restore his vitality. Abishag was exactly what they thought His Majesty needed to get his blood simmering again: tall, voluptuous, with long thick black hair and dark olive skin. But the aged king, with his rotting, wrinkled flesh, was long past his days of chasing beautiful girls and instead needed a good nurse. Abishag, fortunately, excelled as his caretaker, gently soaking the king's sores with warm water, cleaning the mattress (which his body now sometimes soiled), and laying the blankets and pillows just so, so that the arthritic king could find a respite in the soft nest she had built for him.

Solomon loved to watch Abishag at work, but she rarely acknowledged him, and even then usually with a sharp request for a cloth towel or a blanket. Unsure what to do after his failure with the red haired Levite girl, the young prince sat mostly in adoring silence, grateful Abishag was too kind (or too occupied with her duties) to get rid of him.

The besotted boy thought Abishag perfect in every way: not only beautiful, but caring, and so gentle, devoting her every waking thought to finding ingenious ways to make King David more comfortable. For example, Abishag noticed how hard it was for David to stand up and sit down, so she placed objects strategically throughout his suite of rooms, which he could grab and bear weight on as he got up and down, but so stealthily that the old king would feel no shame at being coddled by his nurse.

When Solomon ascended the throne he was sure he would marry Abishag. She would not refuse him—after all, he was now the king of Israel. But then his mother Bathsheba approached him with the news that Adonijah wished to marry Abishag. The new king felt the earth collapse beneath him. Adonijah had challenged Solomon for the throne, and he had only recently routed his brother's supporters. Even though, unlike many of those supporters, Solomon had magnanimously let Adonijah live, he was certain Adonijah was seething with the humiliation of his defeat.

To Solomon, the proposed marriage was clearly a conspiracy, and he raged at his mother for naïvely abetting such base treason. Adonijah was making another run at the throne, he frothed, trying to legitimatize himself by marrying King David's last consort. Perhaps Abishag would now suddenly remember King David expressing a wish for Adonijah to succeed him on the throne.

The plot unfolded clearly in King Solomon's fevered mind. Adonijah was power mad, bloodthirsty, relentless in his efforts to topple and kill his brother, their father's rightful heir and Israel's legitimate monarch. And Abishag too—she too had betrayed him. She had let him sit there like a fool all those hours, letting him think they were friends, when she had been in league with his enemy all along. If Solomon had married her she would have slit his throat in their wedding bed. Just like all those other women, she too was passionate about only beautiful Adonijah. Abishag would surely lie about King David's intentions for the succession to raise her lover up high—all of them would do anything for that lovely face. This treachery must be stamped out, now, quickly, and no more mercy. Dispatching armed guards to slay Adonijah and Abishag, Solomon only relaxed when the soldiers returned with bits of luscious black hair and streaks of blood smattered on their swords.

The ladies of the Jerusalem court were aghast. They had long admired Abishag's unflagging kindness to the ailing King David. Abishag was well known to have long loved Adonijah, and a marriage to the handsome prince, who had retired from politics, seemed a fitting reward for her many good deeds. Yet now the mad—or jealous?—young king had viciously cut down the saintly girl, who had so tenderly nursed his own father.

Solomon thus found the highborn women of Israel more remote than ever. Bodies and voices greeted him stiffly and too correctly. None of them would engage him in conversation, as there was something invariably that needed to be done forthwith—a promised appointment, a need to freshen up. He sighed bitterly, cursing his fate and all of womankind.

The king had tabled the problem of finding a wife while he was preoccupied capturing the *shamir* and imposing the forced labor levy upon the tribes of Israel. But once construction on the Temple was smoothly underway, his thoughts returned again to the problems of marriage, heirs, and the stability of King David's royal line.

With the forced labor imposition having raised tensions between the royal government and the tribes of Israel, especially to the north of Jerusalem, Solomon settled on the notion of marrying a female relation of the leaders of the tribes of Ephraim and Manasseh to shore up support outside his own tribe of Judah. His mother Bathsheba, who had been horrified by the murders of Adonijah and Abishag but hoped that a good wife could check Solomon's cruel impulses, went on a discreet visit to these Northern tribes to arrange the match, but returned home without success. She reported that, while she was received with all appropriate honor due the Queen Mother, the tribes in the north were seething over the forced labor demands for constructing the Temple, and the elders were barely able to contain the discontent in the countryside through impassioned appeals to piety. It was agreed that now was an inopportune time for a marriage alliance, as whoever married his daughter to Solomon would become the symbol of the tyranny of the Jerusalem government, if not worse. Perhaps, Bathsheba concluded, if her son would consider lightening the burden on the men of the north, possibly finding another source of labor for the Temple's construction …

Sitting rigidly on a couch, Solomon did not respond when his mother finished, but glared at her in bitter silence. Bathsheba fidgeted with her bracelets and, turning her eyes away from her son, commented about the poor state of the palace walls, which needed decoration, not to mention something had to be done about the cracks in the paint. Solomon rose. I will have to find a queen another way, he said.

He dreamt of Adonijah that night: Adonijah kissing the petite redhead in the sunset, Adonijah kissing Abishag in the sunset, Adonijah haunting the fantasies of the women of Ephraim and Manasseh swaying in their daydreams on the verandas of their plain stone villas in the northern countryside. Each woman, in his dream, hoped to be Adonijah's bride. As he watched Adonijah's strong hands gently grip each woman's cheeks he could see his brother's head turning to meet Solomon's gaze, with eyes full of contempt for his lonely, weak, ugly brother.

The king of Israel woke, breathing hard. The palace was quiet in the dark night, although a jackal cried somewhere in the distance. The restless king paced about his room, pulsating with rage—he, King Solomon, had finally devoted the monarchy to thanking and glorifying the Holy One, Blessed be He, with a wondrous Temple for Him to dwell in, and the women of the north could think of nothing but their brothers' petty complaints about doing their fair share of the labor. These northerners probably wished Adonijah had won the dynastic struggle—that pretty wastrel would never have had the shrewdness or the discipline to build the Temple. Instead, there would have been parades of drunken revelers with crowns of flowers.

But giving vent to these resentments did not help him solve his problem. None of the appropriate women in Israel, north or south, seemed willing to be his queen. He needed a new approach, perhaps new counsel from a new perspective. If the Israelite women, his mother included, could not find a solution, then the king would have to find wiser advisers. Flanked by soldiers in front and back Solomon once more descended the palace steps to the basement floor and prodded the snoring guards in front of Ashmedai's cell. An embarrassed and groggy man, pulling himself up with some difficulty, fumbled with the lock. After what struck Solomon as too long a delay, the door was finally pushed open.

Ashmedai was sitting, wide awake, on a stool and slowly drawing symbols in the ground with his big toe. His hair and skin still appeared freshly washed and sweetly scented, even though the demon king had never been permitted a bath in the palace, much less access to fine oils and perfumes. While unsure exactly how to broach his difficulty, Solomon was confident this was an area of Ashmedai's expertise: being the chief instigator and nurturer of the *yetzer ha-ra*, the evil impulses of lust and desire, the demon king should have a good understanding of female hearts, or at least a wide range of experience.

Is there any way I may be of assistance to His Majesty on this lovely night? His Majesty rarely visits me, so I must assume this is a serious matter.

Staring at the ground, King Solomon steadied his breathing.

I have another matter upon which I could use your counsel. The matter is royal matchmaking …

The great king of Israel should have no difficulty finding himself a queen. But I suppose you must—why else would you visit?

Ashmedai smirked at the visibly embarrassed Solomon.

Your Majesty must be finding no luck among the fine maidens of Israel. Have you considered a foreign queen? Whatever unpleasant history there is here will not matter to a foreign princess. And the marriage will secure you an alliance with the princess's father, who will bring his troops to your aid if needed. Look at Pharaoh on your western border—he has so many unmarried daughters in need of husbands. I am certain he can spare one for you—and one is really all you need.

Solomon nodded his head. Ashmedai's counsel seemed shrewd—he could secure a queen and an alliance together. If the north was seething with discontent, he could use foreign troops to reinforce his own army. And a foreign queen would have no kinship ties to potential rebels—and no memories of Adonijah's ravishing beauty. Yes, this was quite sensible counsel.

But then he hesitated. Foreign brides meant foreign gods and idolatry, and the wrath of the Holy One, Blessed be He. Could the king whose greatness lay in building the Temple to the Holy One wed a queen who prayed to false gods and creaking idols?

So Solomon put the question to Ashmedai: How can a king of Israel have a queen who bows down to idols? How can I ensure the queen will follow the true path of the Holy One, Blessed be He? His might and His power are greater than Pharaoh's army—as Moses, our teacher, showed long ago.

Letting his gaze linger upon the king for a few moments, Ashmedai ran his fingers through his soft, thick hair, which cascaded lazily over his shoulder onto his chest. That lovely, sweetly scented hair made Solomon's body feel excited and uncomfortable at the same time. He forcibly suppressed these unwelcome sensations.

The demon king responded calmly: What choice do you have? If the Holy One wished a daughter of Israel to wed you, He would have moved her heart towards you. You do not doubt that He has the power to incline one mortal woman's heart in your favor if He really wanted to? It is clearly not His will. I cannot tell you why. The Throne of Glory does not see me as a fit confidante. But His will is what it is, and that is either for you to be a bachelor or to wed a foreign queen. I cannot say which it is. Perhaps the Holy One will speak to you in a dream if you ask Him. But you should respect His will and His design. I am merely trying to help you read the signs and signals that He sends.

Solomon sighed, disturbed by the demon's all too persuasive logic. The king of Israel could not dispute that the Holy One, Blessed be He, could easily move the heart of any lady in Israel, yet apparently chose not to. It could not be that Solomon was fated to be a bachelor—that would be absurd, it would mean civil war over the succession as soon as he was buried in the ground—and how could that be the will of the Throne of Glory? So perhaps it was fated that Solomon would marry a foreign queen.

Maybe, his thoughts continued, this was His plan to strengthen Israel by building foreign military alliances. No doubt the Holy One, Blessed be He, would soften the heart of Solomon's bride, whoever she may be, and reveal enough of His radiance to her, so that she would see the true path and abandon the false gods of her childhood home.

Awake early the next morning, even though he had barely slept, he ordered Benaiah to take a detachment of soldiers and the royal scribe Elihoreph to the court of Pharaoh in Thebes. There Benaiah was to ask, in King Solomon's name, for a bride from among Pharaoh's daughters.

Benaiah stepped back, and, staring at the floor, addressed his king:

Your Majesty, is taking a bride from Egypt wise? The Northerners call you a new Pharaoh who has brought Israel under a new age of bondage. Marrying an Egyptian princess could be seen … there is an expectation that King David's son, like his father, would marry Israelite women, loyal to our Holy One, Blessed be He, and not to false idols of foreign gods. … A girl raised in the sophistication of Egypt, with pleasure cruises on the Nile, to be here, in this still rough place … Has Your Majesty perhaps consulted the Queen Mother?

The Queen Mother failed in her mission. The women of Israel apparently have better men to marry than their king. And we need an alliance with Egypt. The king of Damascus is eager to pick off the north of the kingdom, and he will exploit the resentments of the tribes there. Pharaoh's troops can reinforce our own. We will bind Egypt to us through marriage.

Solomon was certain of his wisdom in this matter—it all made such clear sense—so he held firm and ordered Benaiah to leave that day. In his mind, there stood a graceful, confident Egyptian queen, with delicate floral perfumes wafting from her elegant movements, strolling through Jerusalem in a silk gown, scoffing at the ill-bred ladies of the Israelite court. He cracked a wide, bitter grin at this daydream.

The mission to Pharaoh's court was a success. Benaiah reported his embassy had been hospitably received at Thebes, as the Egyptians were only too pleased to marry off one of their excess princesses to the great King Solomon, promising both a fine dowry and a military alliance.

Quite satisfied with himself, Solomon summoned Bathsheba to inform her curtly that, after her failed mission, he had struck a marriage alliance with a princess of Egypt. The Queen Mother was to arrange for the new queen's suite of apartments and for the wedding festivities. The king offered his gratitude for his mother's assistance in these important affairs of state.

Bathsheba sat down, like a dead bird tumbling down from the sky, and shook her head from side to side. The sun glinted harshly against Solomon's gold necklace, forcing Bathsheba to look away.

As I said, Mother, your gracious help is much appreciated.

He coolly walked out, leaving the trembling Queen Mother by herself.

Pharaoh and King Solomon circulated a joint announcement of the coming marriage, lauding their new alliance and the setting aside of past grievances. A new era of good feelings and brotherhood was dawning between their two peoples. The wedding festivities would be held in Jerusalem in six months' time, with invitations distributed to the leading families of Israel and the neighboring kingdoms.

Various delegations to the royal palace lodged discreet protests—priests, northern elders, retired generals from King David's reign, and so on and so forth. Everyone conceded Solomon's diplomatic shrewdness, but they urged him to consider the awkwardness of a foreign queen—would she understand the demands the Holy One, Blessed be He, uniquely made upon Israel in His Torah and His covenant? Would she eat impure food? Desecrate the Sabbath day? How could she celebrate the rite of Passover, the celebration of Egypt's defeat and Israel's liberation from bondage? Wouldn't she weep for the first born sons of Egypt killed in the final plague? But Solomon summarily dismissed these concerns, confident his new wife would adjust to the ways of the Israelites—and perhaps she could suggest some improvements, too.

The wedding celebration lasted for seven days, with music, dancing, and many clinking toasts and splendid repasts. The king of Israel was triumphant. His bride was all he had dreamed: tall (taller than him), svelte, with high cheekbones, and eyes painted in ovals of dazzling purple. Solomon felt giddy as he saw his bride look with withering disgust upon the court ladies of Jerusalem, with their too strong perfumes and their coarsely woven gowns. A court lady in Jerusalem was the granddaughter of a shepherd and the daughter of a soldier whom King David had elevated to the officer corps. Her so-called nobility was merely an indulgent fiction, a fantasy, equal parts pathetic and presumptuous. But Pharaoh's daughter had a true royal bloodline, which showed in her every poised gesture.

When the time came Solomon eagerly entered his new wife's bed chamber. It was a black night, and the only light in the room was a flickering torch on the wall. There were smoke and sweet fragrances from the bride's tasteful burning of incense to welcome her new husband. Wading through the enchanting fog, he could also smell the oils in which his queen had bathed, and the mix of intoxicating odors made him lightheaded to the point of being almost drunk.

But he stopped suddenly when, around the neck of his bride's invitingly coiled naked body, he saw a necklace holding a small statue. The statue depicted a woman, in Egyptian garb, with a headdress resembling a miniature throne and a small key in one hand, resembling the Egyptian *ankh*, the symbol for life and the key of the Nile. Solomon lurched back.

What is wrong?

The statue, around your neck, who is that?

It is Isis, the goddess who looks after wives. She will bless us and open my womb. By the grace of Isis, we shall have a son.

Isis cannot be here. This is the holy land of Israel. The Holy One, Blessed be He, commanded that He is the Lord Our God who brought us forth from the Land of Egypt, and we shall have no other gods before Him. Isis cannot be here. She defiles this city.

Arching her back like a vicious cat, the Egyptian princess clutched her statue.

I was dedicated to Isis as a little girl, and I would be lost without her protection. How can you spurn the goddess's love so cruelly? She has come to your land to spread peace and fertility. What kind of god of Israel can be so selfish to force you to turn away the blessings Isis offers to all with an open heart?

The royal couple had reached a futile impasse, and avoided each other in the days that followed. The lonely Egyptian queen had friends imported from Egypt, even, if rumors were to be believed, a priestess of Isis, who officiated over secret idolatrous rites in the heart of sacred Jerusalem. The wagging tongues in Jerusalem attributed the queen's childlessness to the wrath of the Holy One, Blessed be He.

Solomon did his best to ignore this scurrilous talk, immersing himself instead in the building of the Temple. Once the dwelling place of the Holy One, Blessed be He, is complete, all will be better, he told himself. My wife will see Him in His Temple, and the vision of His glorious presence will show her that He alone should be her god now.

Thus, shortly after the Temple had been built, he arranged a nocturnal visit with his wife, Pharaoh's daughter. At her husband's insistence the queen left her Egyptian friends behind. Ordering the guards to wait in the outer courtyard, Solomon, brandishing a torch, led the queen into the Temple. The couple walked in silence through the front room. The queen looked around curiously, but her face did not betray her thoughts.

He beckoned her to the inner room, to the Holy of Holies. Once inside the bright golden room, the queen rounded upon the king:

Where is He? If this is His dwelling place, where is His statue?

He cannot be shown in a statue. He is here, He is everywhere here.

The queen burst out laughing.

Your god is nowhere. Stop this foolishness. Lay with me, in the sweet arms of Isis.

Solomon despaired of his lot. Divorce was out of the question, as divorce meant war with Egypt. Nor could he live with Pharaoh's daughter—she would defile his home with foreign idols. So there was no other choice than to build her a separate palace in Jerusalem, where she could discreetly indulge her whims and her foreign goddesses.

The king of Israel ordered that the monthly levy of labor, which had been expected to end with the dedication of the Temple, be reinstated for the construction of the queen's palace. The tribal elders descended upon Jerusalem once more: It was an honor to labor to build a Temple to the Holy One, Blessed be He, but quite another matter to build a palace for a foreign lady who prostrated herself before filthy idols.

But Solomon would brook no dissent. He had promised this palace for his queen. Should her father, the Pharaoh, hear his daughter had been insulted by the Israelites, who would not build her a suitable home, Israel could face war. Would the tribal elders rather have their sons build a palace or fight a bloody war? No one will be killed erecting a palace. The tribal elders acquiesced to Solomon's logic, although he could see the bitterness in their faces. They were bested rather than persuaded.

There were other consequences to Solomon taking an Egyptian bride. The neighboring kings had assumed Solomon would, like his father, draw a wife from among his own people. The news of Solomon's marital alliance with the royal house of Egypt spread alarm throughout the region, leading the petty kings to Israel's north and east to forge hasty alliances with one another. Israel's ambassadors sent urgent dispatches back to Jerusalem: The kingdom's neighbors were scared, he was told, they feared Israel had turned on them in alliance with Egypt.

Solomon was unsure how to respond. There were difficulties everywhere: The Israelites groaned with resentment under their forced labor and their foreign queen, but his foreign queen was disgusted by Solomon's devotion to the invisible Holy One, Blessed be He. And now Israel's neighbors, terrified of the imagined influence of the same foreign queen, were joining together in plots and cabals against him. That famed wise mind turned over his options, but he perceived no ready solution.

In the end, events moved faster than his wise mind: The king of Sidon, glorious metropolis of the Phoenicians to the north, sent an emissary to Jerusalem riding a powerful black horse draped in silver. The rider requested and was granted a prompt audience with the king of Israel.

An uneasy King Solomon thanked the emissary for visiting Jerusalem and praised the wisdom and honor of the great king of Sidon, although he expressed dismay at the difficulty he had encountered arranging foreign travel—so many building projects eating away at him, and so many internal disputes to judge. Nevertheless, he sincerely hoped, someday soon, finally to see the celebrated Sidon. Pray tell, Solomon concluded, what the king of Sidon desires.

The emissary looked at Pharaoh's daughter seated next to her husband and then turned his burning dark eyes to Solomon. He thanked the mighty King of Israel for his hospitality. The Sidonese had always admired the Israelites, and Solomon's wisdom and wealth were renowned across the world. The king of Sidon had long thought that Solomon, like other Israelite kings, would only take a wife from among his own people. This had saddened the king of Sidon, who had a marvelously beautiful and accomplished daughter, a girl whom no one would deserve but a ruler as great as Solomon. The Sidonese court had given up hope of finding a groom worthy of their princess, leading to many sighs lamenting the cruel fate of the dazzling yet lonely princess.

But then word had reached the court at Sidon that King Solomon, may he reign for a hundred years, had wed Pharaoh's daughter. So there was hope, after all, for the forlorn princess. And so, the emissary concluded, the king of Sidon now requested the illustrious and revered King Solomon to be the groom for his daughter, too. Surely such a great king could have no objections to taking a second wife, especially one whose loveliness and grace and wisdom were so wondrous to behold.

The emissary bowed his head again. The Israelites in the throne room looked at Solomon, who turned to his Egyptian queen. She looked, to Solomon's surprise, slouched over with boredom, as her half-closed eyes lingered lazily upon her shoes. He was again unsure what to do. Thanking the emissary for his kind words, the king of Israel said he would take three days to consider the king of Sidon's generous offer. In the meantime, the emissary would be Solomon's guest at the palace. Bathsheba, the lovely and charming Queen Mother, graciously agreed to take the emissary on a tour of the city of Jerusalem and its environs.

Solomon met later that evening, in the parlor room next to his bedchamber, with Benaiah, Bathsheba, and a small group of priests and tribal elders who happened to then be in the capital. He asked their views of the proposal from Sidon: Should he take a second foreign queen?

The advice was unanimous: No. The people were seething with anger, oppressed by forced labor and heavy taxes, and they resented the foreign queen they already had. The priests warned that the Holy One, Blessed be He, would not tolerate even more idol-worshippers in His royal court. Sidon was not worth worrying about. Israel was far mightier, and Israel and Egypt together could easily crush one city. Solomon should refuse the offer, make a face-saving gift instead, and find an Israelite woman to marry, to be the mother to his rightful heir.

Voicing no response, he dismissed them all politely and retired to his bed. The moonlight illuminated the silhouettes of the lions decorating the bed canopy, which looked like ghosts wandering in the night, perhaps confused at the loss of their muscular bodies. These were my father's lions, Solomon reflected. My father, the fearsome King David, was a lion, but I am only the ghost of a lion.

He knew his advisors were right: He was better off avoiding foreign queens and marrying an Israelite lady, who would produce an heir to the throne. An Israelite queen would pray only to the Holy One, Blessed be He, and raise a prince who was pious and kept to His many commandments. Yes, Solomon thought, an Israelite woman is needed.

He thought of the Israelite women of his court, and tried to pick one to approach, but each time he imagined a particular Israelite lady, he saw the ghost of a different lion, of Adonijah with his long mane of hair, materialize in the shadows behind her. Adonijah would lean over, eyes staring at his puny, gangly brother Solomon, and kiss her neck. And the lady would swoon with delight.

Solomon tried to picture the princess of Sidon. Although he had never been to her city, there were, naturally, various Phoenician notables who passed through Jerusalem, some of whom must have been great ladies of the Sidonese court. Yet he could not recall any. So, left with no other recourse, his mind conjured a generic lovely princess, who in truth was the image of Abishag, swathed in a silver dress with light blue makeup applied heavily around her eyes. An Abishag, but more loyal than the real one: this imaginary Abishag of Sidon had never met Adonijah, the wicked traitor and usurper.

Solomon longed for this imaginary princess. It is not right, he told himself, for a great king to be cold and alone in his bed. But he still worried about the trouble that could come with yet another foreign queen.

Jumping up out of bed, he walked to the window to gaze at the full yellow moon. From that vantage point the king could see the Temple he had erected for the glory of the Holy One, Blessed be He, although it appeared a bare dark outline against the night sky. The Temple was a ghost too, Solomon thought, a ghost house for a divinity who would not show His face to contemptuous foreign ladies.

Surrounded by his guards, the sleepless King Solomon descended again to the basement of the palace. When he entered Ashmedai's cell, the demon king, as always perfectly groomed, was standing in a corner singing a hymn to the moon and its beauty. Running his fingers through his thick mane of black hair he asked, ever so softly, what troubled His Majesty at this late hour.

Demon, your advice about the Egyptian princess led to disaster. Your counsel is worthless.

Ashmedai sighed gently.

Your Majesty, my advice was sound. You found a wife, you secured an alliance with Egypt. You soured your marriage by refusing to respect your wife's gods. Did you expect her to love the Holy One, Blessed be He, as you do? You know how He murdered the first born sons of each Egyptian, and drowned that particular unfortunate Pharaoh's army in the sea. Is it any wonder she would rather put her trust in Isis, a goddess who has been loyal and kind to the Egyptians for so many centuries?

Solomon looked down, unsure what to say in response. The demon king continued:

And now I hear the King of Sidon wishes Your Majesty for a son-in-law. You see, there are many demons and demon-helpers still at my command, some as small as flies and spiders. Everything weaves its way back to me in good time. It is not His eyes that always watch you, it is mine. I see you want to marry her, but your people press you to take an Israelite woman. Marry the Sidonese girl. The ladies of Israel have never truly paid you the homage you deserve, and they will never forgive you for killing Adonijah and Abishag. Do you want to lay with a queen whose mind will plot against you, who waits for just the moment to slip a draught of poison to revenge sweet Abishag? A foreign princess is much better. She will not care about your traitor brother whom you had to put down—believe me their fathers and brothers have done much worse—and they will need to rely upon you for protection in a hostile, foreign land. And you will secure alliances with kings with their own armies, in case Adonijah's example proves tempting again to one of the noble members of your court. My counsel is wise, I am older than the human race, and I will be here still when you are finally all turned back to dust again.

Ashmedai grinned, baring teeth that were blinding in their whiteness and pointed and sharp, like an animal's fangs.

At a loss for words, Solomon quietly left the demon king's cell, and wound his way back up to his bed, feeling firm in his decision to reject the king of Sidon's offer of a marriage alliance. A new foreign queen would only sow new resentments in the land and tempt the just wrath of the Holy One, Blessed be He by bringing in more foreign gods, more filthy idols, into His holy capital in His promised land.

That night was unseasonably cold and a rain storm fell from the skies, unleashing a powerful wind, which ripped away his blanket and splattered cold rain on his royal person. Solomon woke with a start, sure his end had come: secret plotters, who had never accepted him as King David's legitimate heir, allies of Adonijah out to avenge his cruel death, had stolen into the king's room, grabbed his blankets, and were now ready to run him through with their daggers. The king of Israel began to mumble prayers of repentance and confession to the Holy One, Blessed be He.

But soon Solomon's mind cleared, and he yearned for a soothing caress of his cheek and a light whisper of sympathy to ease him through the storm, which had left him uncovered and shivering and wet. Recalling how Abishag had comforted the frail, dying King David on such long winter nights, he smoldered with envy and hatred. Was he so awful that he did not merit such simple, gentle tenderness, too? Why was he abandoned by the women of Israel, left alone in his bed to twitch in the wet cold like an abandoned dog in an alley?

Solomon thought of the unmarried women who milled about his court, both young maidens and elegant, reserved widows. As he summoned each face, he recalled how that lady was so stiff and uncomfortable when forced to address her king, or how that one's body kept drifting away from him, as if seeking an ocean current to save her from the king's loathsome presence. And always the parade of appropriate excuses when he invited these noble ladies to dine or meet with him privately—sick loved ones, long-planned journeys, an emergency with the servants in a country estate—it was always one thing or another, but the end result of all those unimpeachable words was the king shivering pathetically in his drenched nightgown, alone in his palace bedroom in the night.

He cursed the women of Israel. Was he so horrible? He was not a monster. He could murder half the kingdom at his whim, but he did nothing of the sort. He had devoted his energies to building the great Temple for the Holy One, Blessed be He, where those same ladies piously intoned their supplications and flaunted their virtue with conspicuously abundant sacrifices.

Solomon so painfully craved a tender caress and a soft soothing whisper in the cold, rainy night. If the bitter Israelite ladies would not show this simple decency to their king, then he would find such human goodness elsewhere, from a foreign country, from a princess who did not harbor lingering sentiments about Adonijah and Abishag.

At the appointed time, King Solomon summoned the emissary from Sidon to the parlor outside his bedchamber and accepted the marriage proposal of the King of Sidon. The emissary was appropriately grateful. His advisors looked at each other with wide, frantic eyes.

This second royal wedding took place in due course. To Solomon's surprise, the Egyptian princess was excited at his taking a second wife. While Bathsheba groped for excuses to delay and belabor the wedding preparations, Pharaoh's daughter swooped in and took command of the planning, using her connections with the Egyptian royal court to import the necessary luxuries and delicacies.

This time Solomon swore he would not let himself be bothered by a stray idol. Ashmedai was right, he thought, I do need to learn to be more tolerant and forgiving. Yet when he saw the statue of the goddess Asherah hanging from his new foreign bride's neck, he simply could not touch her. The idol's cold eyes filled him with longing for the warmth of the enveloping mist of the Holy One, Blessed be He.

Taking a second foreign wife had further consequences for King Solomon and his capital. Neighboring kings now became convinced he was cementing a multi-state military alliance through these marriages, leading each petty princeling to be scared at being left out and isolated militarily. So princess after princess was offered up to Solomon in marriage—Ammonite, Moabite, Hittite, and so on and so forth. Solomon felt little choice but to accept, as he did not wish to offend a nearby king and thereby precipitate an unnecessary war. Anyway, he thought, what difference does one more bride make?

Jerusalem was soon overrun with foreign queens. With their households and priests and priestesses and servants and wardrobes and furniture, the many foreign princesses could not be contained within the existing, modest palace. So Solomon was compelled to continue the forced levy of the young men of the tribes of Israel, who now found themselves, during their monthly turns, slave laborers erecting pleasure villas for their king's unfortunate collection of haughty, idol-worshipping foreign brides.

While forbidding the public worship of any god but the Holy One, Blessed be He, he permitted the foreign queens to erect private shrines inside their houses to their foreign idols. His advisors had angrily opposed this act of leniency, but Solomon feared the diplomatic repercussions if the neighboring monarchs felt their daughters and priests and gods were treated too rudely by the Israelites. As long as their rites were discreetly hidden away, the king of Israel reasoned he could maintain both his foreign alliances and Israel's piety.

From his bedchamber window he could sometimes see the smoke and smell the fragrance of the incense burning inside the various palaces of his many different queens. The smell filled his spirit with a lightheaded longing for a soft feminine love. But he could not bring himself to embrace a woman surrounded by, even wearing upon her body, idols of false gods.

The foreign princesses soon formed their own society in Jerusalem, as, having no ties to Israel's court or to its God, they found better company in each other. Nevertheless, some of Israel's wealthier citizens became curious about this secret society of mysterious, beautiful foreign queens with their sorcerer priests and witch priestesses, especially when wild rumors circulated of excesses of carnal pleasure and dark, powerful magic. So some Israelites were tempted to peek into the foreign queens' palaces and even to pray—just for the sake of politeness, just for the sake of being a good guest—at the shrines of Isis and Asherah, of Baal and Molech.

Other Israelites were less welcoming of Jerusalem's foreign colony. King Solomon's mother, Bathsheba, disgusted by the tales spread of Solomon's wives, retired to a villa in the countryside. Benaiah was forced to travel the land with cohorts of soldiers to put down one small rebellion after another—the forced labor levy and the taxes demanded for the upkeep of all these foreign queens had made the people, especially in the north, simmer with a rage that all too easily exploded into short, disorganized bursts of bloody insurrection.

IV. The Devil and the King Conspire to Cheat the Angel of Death

WITH HIS TROUBLES mounting, King Solomon now often retreated into his private suite of rooms in the palace, where he would pass the time by setting himself mathematical problems of ever greater complexity. But eventually, one such problem turned out to be so convoluted that he was not sure how to solve it. After stomping and cursing and pulling his hair in ever mounting hopeless frustration, he ultimately decided to summon his old schoolmate and scribe, Elihoreph, for help.

Elihoreph, a wisp of a man with painfully near-sighted eyes and a wheezing chest, was able to work carefully through the problem, showing the king he had made a slight error in its premise. Seeing how he had driven himself into a thundering fury by such a simple error, Solomon laughed indulgently at his own vain folly. Although Elihoreph looked at him uncomfortably, he could not help himself, he simply had to laugh at that moment, as he found himself, and his self-imposed solitude, and the indignant pagan harpies he had wed, and the frothing rebels in the northern tribes, to all be just too funny, for some inexplicable reason.

King Solomon urged Elihoreph to be at ease: You have brought joy to me, at long last. Come, sit down, let's talk. It has been too long.

At Solomon's request, a servant brought a jug of wine, two cups, and a plate of dried figs and almonds. Feeling the calming effects of the wine, the king of Israel lay back on the couch and asked Elihoreph how he had been faring of late.

Elihoreph drank a cup of wine in one quick gulp before launching into a surprisingly long and angry speech—about the royal budget and, in particular, corrupt procurement officers who overpaid for building supplies. Comparing the records of transactions registered in the palace accounting ledgers with inquiries he had made to ascertain prevailing market prices revealed a discrepancy so large and inexplicable it could only be the residue of corruption. If these goods had been purchased at fair market value, then sufficient funds could be freed to upgrade the army's older chariots, or at least a few of them.

Especially the axles on those chariots. Elihoreph was convinced King David's engineers had done a miserable job of designing chariot axles. They were limited in their weight-bearing so the chariot could only carry two riders—a soldier to steer the horses and a soldier to fight. But a different axle design would allow a three-man crew, which could attack simultaneously from both sides.

This diatribe spewed forth with barely a pause to breathe. Elihoreph seemed completely ignorant of the idolatrous rites of the pagan princesses, or of the simmering discontent in the countryside. To him, all the woes of Israel came down to poor management of the purchasing of timber and tallow and, even more, to incompetent design of chariot axles. Solomon mused that Elihoreph had managed to rearrange the vicious world into an innocent fairytale of accounting and engineering.

Delighted to let himself tumble into Elihoreph's mental world, the king of Israel leaned towards his friend and asked questions about both the prices of building materials and the axle design. Elihoreph's eyes sparkled. In his glee, he stood up from the couch and shook his hands rapidly as he declaimed further on his favorite subjects.

Although Solomon subsequently gave Elihoreph a special mandate both to reform the procurement process and to redesign the standard Israelite army chariot, he did not really care whether Elihoreph was able to make a difference in these areas, or even if the problems identified were real. With Elihoreph, he was at last able to forget his troubles fomented by both the supporters and opponents of his odious wives. As there was not enough royal business to fill their increasingly frequent meetings in the king's palace apartments, the two friends often played chess. Losing himself in the game for hours, although he did not care if he won or lost (and in fact he lost more often than he won), what King Solomon enjoyed was the sensation that there was nothing in the universe except these little wooden game pieces warily circling and attacking each other on the board.

And then a strange illness interrupted his idyll with Elihoreph. For a couple of weeks Elihoreph's wheezing chest had been worse than normal. The royal court physician attempted to help, but his remedies proved fruitless. Still, Solomon told himself not to worry: Elihoreph is young, it is just a bad chill on his lungs, give it some time and all will be well.

But the chill would not release its grip. When Elihoreph became too weak to pay visits to the palace, the king took to visiting his lodgings instead. Being a reclusive bachelor, Elihoreph needed little space—a bed, a wash basin, a small table—really just a room, which was located in a modest villa in a neighborhood far from the palace. The area was filled with winding alleyways, rickety houses, and makeshift stalls for goats and chickens. Its residents trudged heavily about in wrinkled, stained robes, their voices alternating between self-absorbed mutters and furious explosions of cursing at one another.

King Solomon was not expected in that part of Jerusalem. Escorted by armed guards on all sides, his household slaves carried him in a litter; its thick blue curtains blocked the unpleasant scenery. Nevertheless, the smells—animal droppings on the street, sweaty men who rarely bathed, stale, damp clothes taking too long to dry in the stale air—seeped into Solomon's traveling box and cut through the perfumes in his hair, boring into his nose against his will.

After his troops cleared the front of the building, Solomon would have his litter lowered right in front of the door. Once inside it was a quick walk to Elihoreph's room, which opened to the left of the main hallway. The landlady, a beaming old woman in a brightly colored head scarf, would bring Elihoreph and his famous guest freshly brewed herbal teas made from chamomile flowers, sometimes adding a touch of honey.

King Solomon soon noticed something unusual on these visits to his sick friend. There would appear, in the corner of his eye, a pale man who was so tall he was forced to stand stooped over. Around the belted waist of the man's hooded black robe dangled a long knife with a wooden handle. Oblivious to his surroundings, this man was continually scrutinizing a piece of papyrus he held in his spidery hands.

Elihoreph did not seem to notice the man. Nor did the landlady, or any of the palace guards who would sometimes enter. King Solomon would worry he had caught a terrible disease from Elihoreph, which was causing him to hallucinate this waxen apparition. Still, no matter how he struggled to suppress the image, Solomon invariably saw this man there at each visit, in his corner quietly preoccupied with his papyrus.

One afternoon, when the two friends were alone, Elihoreph drifted off to sleep, his slowing, receding voice finally swallowed up by the need for rest. Taking Elihoreph's limp hand in his own, Solomon sighed and stroked his friend's damp, hot hair. And once again, stooped in the corner, was the pale hooded man with his long knife.

At that moment, overcome with a sudden, inexplicable loathing for the apparition, who was continually eavesdropping on his intimate moments, Solomon walked over to the mysterious man, so close that his nose almost collided with the stooped man's lips. But the apparition did not appear to notice Solomon, remaining, as always, silently absorbed in the study of the papyrus scroll in his hand.

Solomon grabbed the papyrus. Written on it were ten names, including Elihoreph's. A hand grabbed the papyrus back. The waxen face stared at Solomon in terror, as if he had just noticed his presence and thought the king of Israel was the unsettling ghost. Another hand hit Solomon across the face. Everything went dark.

When the king of Israel came around, he found himself lying in the opposite corner of Elihoreph's room. There was no sign of the stooped man or his papyrus, and Elihoreph was snoring softly on the bed. Seeing that night had fallen, Solomon returned home to the palace.

But he could not sleep. Summoning a royal scribe, he dictated the list of names from the stooped man's papyrus, as best he could recall them. Except for Elihoreph, the names were not familiar to him, although they all sounded Israelite. Solomon's body grew steadily colder when he read over the names recorded by the scribe, even though it was a warm night.

The next morning royal inquiries were made into the names on the list. Now and again the stooped man lurked in the corner of Solomon's eye, but there turned out to be no one when he turned his head. Throughout the day the king lost track of what was said to him, forgot the purpose of different audiences, and seemed to have offended an ambassador from somewhere because he could not recall something, or someone, important to that emissary's king and his border dispute with some other monarch arising from the disputed inheritance of their common ancestor, who once ruled some other kingdom. It all seemed too confusing and pointless.

The world was a muddle of faint, far off background noise, as if Solomon were watching someone else's day unfold on a stage. The details of decay appeared everywhere: paint peeling on walls, slight scratches on his plates, food that tasted stale, and wine that reeked of vinegar. Everything seemed to be past its prime and glory, slipping back into its original, unformed raw state. He felt an oppressive sadness, not from nostalgia or longing, but owing to the absence of vitality everywhere he looked.

Benaiah entered the royal bedchamber, interrupting Solomon's brooding thoughts.

What news? The king asked.

Your majesty, the names, the list of names you gave. It is a list of … well … a list of … the recently deceased.

How do you mean?

Every name but Elihoreph is the name of someone from Jerusalem who died in the past week. They lived near Elihoreph, all within easy walking distance of his home. We thought their deaths must be connected because … because they were on your list together. But they did not know each other. And they all died differently. One died of old age, another an infant who died of a fever, a third was trampled by an angry donkey. The only thing we can say about the names is that they all died, and died recently, here in Jerusalem. If I may ask, where did Your Majesty get this list?

Solomon staggered back on his couch, feeling a sharp stab of pain in his abdomen. After looking anxiously at the silent king for several minutes, Benaiah excused himself on the grounds that he had to set out for Ashkelon to see to the kingdom's defenses against a naval attack. Solomon nodded his head, but did not look up.

Hastily summoning the priests to the Temple, the king ordered the sacrifices of many bulls and goats to the Holy One, Blessed be He. He prayed: Lord my God, King of the

Universe, please rescind the harsh decree of Your heavenly tribunal and spare Elihoreph. Your poor, humble servant Solomon needs this man, needs this man to help him rule Your people and Your kingdom. Please, I beg You, come to me in my dream tonight. Let me speak to You so that I may plead Elihoreph's case. He is a righteous soul.

But that night the Holy One, Blessed be He, did not come to King Solomon in his dream. Nor did Elihoreph's health improve but, to the contrary, worsened to the point that he could barely eat. Solomon was too scared to return to his friend—scared of that waxen face in the black robe with his glinting knife—but sent messengers back and forth multiple times each day.

The news was grim, but he insisted on hearing each new report, no matter how dreadful. He dispatched the royal court physicians to his dying friend, who dutifully examined the patient, compared notes, and debated diagnoses. Yet each one reached the same conclusion: The case was hopeless, so it was best simply to smooth Elihoreph's passage into the World to Come by easing his pain.

Solomon turned to his soothsayers and prophets. Tell me, he demanded, how can we save Elihoreph? He is a righteous man, a good man, and his suffering is unjust. The soothsayers and prophets cast their spells and burned incense and summoned angels to answer King Solomon. In the end, they too spoke with one voice: The decree has come down from the Throne of Glory, this is the will of the Holy One, Blessed be He, accept it and rejoice that Elihoreph will soon join the other righteous men of Israel in the eternal bliss of Paradise.

Solomon seethed: how could the Holy One, Blessed be He, do this to him? He had built the magnificent Temple in Jerusalem, and he had refused to touch any of his foreign wives because their lovely lithe forms were swathed in the grotesque images of their false idols. The king had been faithful to the Holy One, Blessed be He, and had worshipped no other gods before Him. So how could the Holy One rob him of the one comfort he had in this world? Was it the will of the Holy One that Solomon was to be alone on his throne, bereft of any friend to ease his burdens? Why did the king of Israel not merit a scrap of indulgent kindness from the Throne of Glory?

And what of Elihoreph's suffering? Elihoreph was an honest, sweet soul. It was all well and good to daydream about him skipping through orange groves in sun-dappled Paradise, holding hands with the matriarchs Rachel and Leah, but here, now, Elihoreph was writhing in terrible misery in a worn, damp bed in a foul manure-ridden corner of Jerusalem. The Holy One's way was the wrong way, Solomon decided. There must be another solution—the king was convinced his cleverness could outwit the decree against Elihoreph.

He descended once more to the basement of the palace. The trip down the winding staircase was particularly dark, as whoever was supposed to do so had not bothered to light the wall torches, so that the interior stairway was lit only by the dim candle held by the guard in front. Barely able to see, the king of Israel would have tripped if his guards were not pressed so tightly against him that the burly men steadied their shaking, gangly lord. One guard's sword flickered in the faint light, looking like an uncanny replica of the stooped man's long knife.

The light was better when they reached the basement landing. Although once again the wall torches were neglected, a light, bright and white and almost blinding, burst from the slender crack underneath the door to Ashmedai's cell. Rejoicing at this light, Solomon pushed aside the guards in front of him to thrust open the demon king's door, although he did not ask himself how it had become unlocked. Inside the cell Ashmedai stood in a corner, relaxed, with his thick, lavender-scented hair falling carelessly over his shoulder. The light seemed to emanate from the demon himself, as there were no candles or torches lit in his cell.

How can I be of assistance to Your Majesty? Your visits to me are so rare. It can be lonely to be your prisoner.

Demon, do you know the stooped man in the black robe with the knife? He stalks my friend's room. My friend's sickbed. How do I ward him off?

Ashmedai shook his head gently. You men make far too much of him. He is a messenger. He is told the decree of the Throne of Glory, then dispatched with his knife to carry it out. You do not ward him off. He is not one of my imps you can scare away with an amulet and a spell.

Groping unsuccessfully for a response, Solomon looked down at the floor as the hot white light had begun to hurt his eyes, making him dizzy and nauseous. The king of the demons broke the silence:

You cannot ward him off, but you can escape him. The stooped man and his knife can roam far and wide, but he cannot enter the city of Luz. This is the city of eternal life. And not the eternal life of the World to Come, but true eternal life, endless physical real life, life with air and wine and spiced roasted meat. When Adam and Eve disobeyed the Holy One and brought death into the world, He decided there should be a refuge for the righteous on Earth, and so He made the city of Luz. It is hidden in a mist, and its walls have no gates, so you have not only to find the city, but to know where the great hollow tree is whose trunk is the secret passageway into Luz.

In Luz, everything delights the senses: the air smells of fresh flowers, there is abundant wine and mead, and everyone dines on fresh, tender cuts of meat three times a day. There are no marriages in Luz, because who could commit for an unending eternity? So men and women roll in bed with each other at their whim, savoring the eternally youthful pink flesh of each one of their neighbors.

Some of my demons know the way to Luz. If you like, Your Majesty, I can summon one. She will spirit your friend away to safety there. He will regain his strength and health in Luz, and then some. We will ferry you, too, over to Luz in good time to visit him.

Just ask, and I will see that it is done.

But why would you do this for me? What good would it do you?

Your Majesty, unlike the Holy One, I appreciate your suffering—your feckless wives, your rebellious subjects, the demands, the petitions, the plots cropping up here and there and everywhere. As one king to another, I am happy to assist you in your time of need. And what do you risk? Do nothing and the pale ghost's long knife will shortly sever your friend from this world, and you will lose him. At least this is some hope.

Ashmedai's logic made sense to Solomon: What could he lose? Until this moment, no one had offered any hope for saving Elihoreph. As a true and loyal friend, he owed it to Elihoreph to try. And the king of Israel imagined a heartfelt reunion with a newly healthy Elihoreph in Luz, drinking wine, chewing seasoned goat meat on a skewer, and swapping suggestions for chariot axle designs with nine-hundred-year-old saints.

I agree. Summon your demon.

Ashmedai quickly mumbled words in a language Solomon did not understand, although the words sounded gentle and lyrical, with soft consonants and nasal vowels, which made a pleasing contrast to the guttural harshness of Israelite Hebrew. A creature soon appeared in between Ashmedai and Solomon, with the head of a woman, the body of a lion, and birds' wings and feet, including great curved claws. Looking puzzled, it craned its neck towards the demon king.

Your Majesty, again, the name of your friend?

Elihoreph.

Go to Elihoreph and take him safely to Luz. Do it now, disregard your other duties.

The creature nodded and flew off.

Solomon returned to his bedchamber, where he joyously toasted the shining moon with a cask of sweet wine in celebration of having finally saved his friend. Drifting into sleep, he dreamed of Luz: a paradise filled with sunshine, eternally young and game beautiful women, sweet fruit, wine, roasted meat, and an endless lazy, sensual idyll. There, in a corner of the city, Elihoreph wore a light blue and orange striped robe as he was speaking to a group of alluring women. Solomon began to walk towards them.

A clamor outside the window woke him. Although it was morning already, he had not fallen asleep until close to dawn, so he still lacked a proper rest. Summoning his steward, Solomon gave word that he felt slightly ill, nothing dangerous, but the king would need to cancel his morning appointments. He fell back asleep after dismissing the servant.

For a time, everything was calm and dark and empty in this renewed sleep. But then a new dream formed. Solomon was now in his throne room, wearing a dark purple robe and his jewel-studded diadem. The room was empty, but he found this solitude to be a comfort.

The throne room doors then swung open, and in walked a tall stooped man, taller than Solomon by far, in a hooded black robe with a long knife swinging on his belt. The man kneeled before King Solomon, who asked him to rise and state his business.

Standing up again, the man reached halfway to the high vaulted ceiling, and his knife grew to monstrous proportions. The room went dark except for a dull bluish light, which illuminated the man's impassive waxen face. He stated his business in a flat tone:

I bring greetings and a message to Your Esteemed Majesty, the King of Israel, from the King of Kings seated on the most exalted Throne of Glory in the World to Come. The Holy One, Blessed be He, is not pleased with your attempts to interfere with His decrees. He and He alone can write the entries in the Book of Life and the Book of Death. No one is permitted to interfere, not me, and certainly not you.

Elihoreph, may his memory be for a blessing, is safely in Paradise in the World to Come, where he reclines upon a soft couch learning the secrets of wisdom at the Celestial Academy. You are not the first man to try to trick me. I have a guard stationed inside the hollow trunk that is the passageway between this earthly world, where I may roam, and the city of Luz, where I cannot enter. I was summoned after my guard heard Elihoreph's approach. Your dear friend was a pitiful sight: coughing, wheezing, shaking, his wrecked physical husk torturing the lovely sweet soul trapped inside. Yet he was alert enough to know he was being carried in the terrible claws of the winged monster you sent to him. The monster's sweat stank of sulfur, the perfumes of *Gehenna*, of Hell. Elihoreph's eyes were filled with a terror that his soul had somehow been damned to the realm of demons. Seeing me and my guard, he visibly relaxed. We pulled Elihoreph from the creature's claws and shooed it away. I took Elihoreph outside the tree and put him to sleep, before driving my knife into him to cut out his soul and ferry it to the World to Come. He felt no pain.

There are two reasons, Your Majesty, why I have a guard stationed inside the large hollow tree trunk outside Luz. The first, as I mentioned, is to catch men trying to evade the decrees of the Throne of Glory. There are not many of these. Luz is hard to find, and most men have enough piety to submit to the will of the Holy One, Blessed be He.

The second reason is to help the poor souls fleeing Luz in terror. Do you think this city is some sort of paradise? True Paradise, the Garden of Eden, is in the World to Come and only admits pure and righteous souls. Luz is a terrible place. The only difference between Luz and the outside world is my absence. The residents of Luz grow old, wrinkled, hobbled, crippled, and sick, but they cannot die. They are tightly confined with the same companions for centuries, overfamiliarity has bred hatred and resentment and grudges to the point that each resident of Luz is isolated in his suspicion of everyone else in that abysmal city. The weather is brutal: freezing rains and winds that chill those old, cracking bones. There is nothing that can grow in Luz's never-ending winter. The eternal city's eternal residents are tortured with hunger, constant hunger, along with continual pounding headaches and knotting pains.

The Holy One, Blessed be He, built this city for an evil race. Before the Flood, before righteous Noah, may his memory be a blessing, the *Nephilim* had descended to Earth and had lain with human women. They gave birth to a race of powerful giants, half human and half angel, who roamed the Earth and took whatever tickled the fancy of their senses. These brutes gave themselves over fully to the *yetzer ha-ra*, the evil inclination, leading humanity into the sinful state that the Flood cleansed.

I was dispatched to take them into the next world. I was young then, having only been born in Heaven at the moment when Adam and Eve ate the fruit of the Tree of Knowledge of Good and Evil—I was the seedling of the apple they plucked, which sprouted and grew in the upper realms. I went with my knife to take these giants away, but they fought me off.

So the Holy One, Blessed be He, made the city of Luz, where I was forbidden to enter. And He came to the wicked giants in a pillar of fire and told them they had a choice: They could wait until they became too old and weak to resist my knife, or they could leave humanity alone and live forever in Luz, where I could not go. These gluttons were terrified of losing the pleasures of their insatiable bodies, and so they tramped off to Luz. The only way in or out—the tree—was too small for them, leaving them trapped. These are the residents of Luz, who have suffered terribly, but justly, for their many sins.

Sometimes, though, in old age, their bodies have shrunk sufficiently so that they are able to crawl into the hollow of the tree, where they beg my guard to summon me, to release their souls. I pity these miserable creatures. I release their souls from their wrinkled, crippled husks. Purified of sin by hundreds of years of suffering, their souls ascend meekly and humbly to the gates of Paradise.

Solomon, King of Israel, do not interfere again. Your throne is not the Throne of Glory. You were made from the dust, and you will return to the dust. Tempt His mercy again and perhaps your name will be added to my list. You are all maggots to me.

Solomon woke with a start. The bedroom and the sunlight and the breakfast platter left discreetly on a nearby table all seemed unreal to him. The walls spun madly around and it took all of the king's powers of concentration to steady himself. With a focused effort he rose, dressed, ate, and dove into his daily business.

But in every corner there seemed to be a stooped, angry man in a black cloak. The figure would begin to form to the side, in the far corner of the king's line of sight. He would try to ignore it, tell himself he was being ridiculous, but he also started to feel a chill, even though everyone else in the room appeared perfectly comfortable. The chill continued to creep up his legs and wrapped itself tightly around his body. Solomon's heart pounded violently. He tried to distract himself by focusing on the details of whatever petition was being presented—the description of the stolen property, the distinguishing marks on an injured man—and he questioned the parties feverishly, relentlessly—allowing no point to be overlooked.

But the chill would coil ever more tightly around his unsteady frame. Sure that the stooped man was close, long knife drawn and ready to gut his rickety body, Solomon could no longer resist turning in the direction he had willed himself to avoid, where he now saw—nothing. Gradually his muscles would relax, and the king of Israel would stop questioning the parties before him, letting their staccato reproaches to one another float over his exhausted, numb soul.

Yet this peace of mind would not last long. Solomon would soon enough again see the stooped man in the corner of his eye, and the same painful cycle would repeat itself. His advisors grew concerned about the king's erratic swings from manic engagement to mute absence, and there were gentle suggestions of the need for rest and perhaps a quick visit from the royal physician, just as a precaution, as His Majesty seemed slightly unwell.

No, Solomon insisted, my health is sound, and the business of my subjects is of the utmost importance. They are each entitled to a fair and thorough hearing and a just decision. We must continue. We shall not rest until we have done our duty.

The king of Israel did not notice how sharp and loud his voice had become, or the way he shivered as he spoke.

After one such terror-stricken day, Solomon sat alone in his bed chamber, unable to sleep even though he was worn out from the wild swings of his nerves. The flickering shadows on the wall swayed and taunted him in the shape of a stooped, hooded man. The king leapt to his feet and turned quickly to look in each direction.

The room was empty.

He lay back down, but his eyes would not close. Perhaps I am losing my wits, he thought. Perhaps that is the stooped man's game. I am now on his list—there must be some dreadful punishment for trying to thwart his work. And to go under that long knife seems a fitting rebuke—but he will not let me go easily. His plan is to drive me mad. The stooped man will wink at me from the shadows and slither away, appear and hide, again and again, to make me mad, and to make me doubt what is real. Life will be unbearable. He wants me to pray, to beg for death, as a release from this torture.

Or to kill myself—yes, that is it. The stooped man wants me to kill myself. The Holy One, Blessed be He, has forgiven me in His great mercy and has not decreed my death. So the stooped man cannot do what he wants to do himself. But he can make me so crazed with terror that I will do his wretched deed for him.

Solomon screamed aloud: I will not let him! I will not let him! I am king and I shall live!

The guards rushed in. Was His Majesty safe? Was there an intruder threatening? We see no one.

The king of Israel forced himself to appear calm. You are right, no one has been here and there is no one to see. Leave me, I need to rest. It must have been a dream.

The guards dutifully filed out of the room.

Once he was alone again, Solomon walked over to the window to gaze at the night sky and inhale the cool night air. Everything seemed peaceful in the shadows of the sleeping city.

He looked down. The drop from the window was forbidding, and a fall would likely be fatal. One moment of weakness, a panicked jump, and the stooped man gets his underhanded victory.

King Solomon swore to himself he would not let it happen. He needed to break free of the stooped man, to drive him away. But how?

Tapping his fingers against the window ledge, he stared out at the stars and pondered his fate, until, after lingering for some time, he once again descended to the palace basement. Inside his cell, Ashmedai slouched in a corner on a pile of hay, humming a tune and running his long fingers through his thick, perfumed black hair.

Can I be of assistance to Your Majesty? Your Grace appears unwell. Perhaps you would like to rest? This hay is soft, and you can lay your head here, right by me.

Ashmedai cocked his head to the side and arched his eyebrows slightly. The gesture struck Solomon as oddly flirtatious, unsettling him even further.

Demon king, I need the power to resist the stooped man in the black robe and his knife. I need to expel him from my land, or at least from my presence. He is bent on driving me mad. Do you have this power? Can you resist him? Expel him? You were there when he was born. You must know how to ward him off.

Certainly I know. You don't see him coming after me, do you? Or any of my demon subjects? But ...

Ashmedai lifted his hands and thrust his golden chains forward, on which Solomon saw inscribed the true hidden names of the Holy One, Blessed be He. The sight of the holy names hurt his eyes and made his temples throb violently.

But I cannot muster that power while I am shackled. If you desire such weighty secrets, I need to be freed, and I will need your signet ring.

Without thinking Solomon complied. He unfastened the chains and threw them under a pile of hay. He was desperate to be spared the painful sight of the holy names. Blood gingerly trickled from his finger where he had so hastily ripped off his signet ring.

Once Ashmedai had placed the signet ring on his finger, he grabbed hold of Solomon in his arms, growing larger and larger until he towered over the human king. Solomon felt, at that moment, comfortable and safe, as if Ashmedai were his merciful father, who would love and protect him.

The two were transported outside the palace under the night sky, where a red, sulfurous cloud drifted over them. Solomon felt himself being tossed into that cloud; the vapors seared his skin. The cloud took off at a terrifying speed, lurching up and down, to the left and to the right, making the king of Israel vomit all over himself in the midst of these mad gyrations.

The cloud slowed gradually and finally descended gently to the ground where it dissipated. Solomon felt the comfort of hard dirt under his body. His clothes were tattered and stained with his vomit and he shook involuntarily. It was still nighttime, and the king was in the middle of a wide dirt road. He thought he saw lights in the distance—a city perhaps?

The king of Israel, in rags and filth, with his head throbbing, hobbled towards the lights.

V. The Beggar King

AS KING SOLOMON reached the city around dawn, weather-beaten men and women were trudging with carts loaded with produce through the open gates. The city was modest in scale. There were narrow alleyways to his left and right lined with tightly packed, small wooden houses. In the distance, a hill was visible with imposing stone villas, no doubt the neighborhood of the local rich. He followed the carts down the smoothly paved main street, careful to avoid the animal droppings on the ground.

The procession of carts stopped in a square in front of an austere temple. The steps led up to a circular landing with an altar and an elegant green marble statue of a great bull. Solomon knew then he was no longer in Israel, and he had been exiled from the dwelling place of the Holy One, Blessed be He.

A yawning, portly man in a pink silk robe ascended the steps and stationed himself by the altar. One by one various people took animals from their carts—mostly small pigs—

and brought them up for sacrifice. The bull god's priest pronounced his benediction, slaughtered each little pig and burned its entrails, while putting aside a portion for himself.

The stench of the roasting pig meat, an unclean animal forbidden to the people of Israel, made Solomon sick and unsteady. At the sight of the idol of the bull god looking out with cold sculpted eyes upon his subservient people, the lost king of Israel was overcome with loneliness and yearned for the Holy One, Blessed be He, to envelop him in His pillar of smoke and to whisk him home.

He knelt down, closed his eyes, and prayed with all his heart to the Holy One, Blessed be He, to return to Jerusalem. He promised to rid the city of idols, even to rid the city of its foreign queens. He would do away with Ashmedai. He would marry any Israelite girl, even a water carrier's daughter, just so he could dwell once more in the land of the Holy One, Blessed be He, and His people Israel.

The crowd slowly thinned out as the various idol worshippers made their offerings and received their blessings. The groggy priest appeared ever more perfunctory in his duties, doubtless skipping over portions of his prayers. Even the bull god's eyes seemed to glaze over with boredom in the glare of the morning sun.

But no mist or cloud or messenger from the Holy One, Blessed be He, came to rescue Solomon. He simply stood by himself, covered in the caked filth of his tracks of vomit, and stared mutely at the foreign idol and the tottering pile of dead pigs.

The priest had finished his duties, signaling to someone—a servant? A priest of inferior rank?—to take away the portions of the sacrificial offerings that had been set aside for the bull god's priesthood. Stretching his arms and scratching his armpit, the self-satisfied priest headed slowly back down the temple steps.

Solomon was seized by a terrible fear that the bull god would come to life and gore him for his lack of respect for his wives' idols. But he told himself not to be afraid: He was the great King Solomon, mighty lord of Israel, and great kings do not cower in fear, but instead display their natural superiority. So he strode confidently toward the priest, whose sleepy eyes filled him with such contempt that King Solomon indignantly began issuing commands:

Priest, I am Solomon, King of Israel. Where is this land? I command you to return me to my country at once. Summon my ambassador immediately. Preparations must be made.

The priest stared at Solomon for a moment, chuckled to himself, and then walked off in the direction of a side road. Solomon followed him, continuing to shout orders: The King of Israel needs his chariot! And a retinue of soldiers for protection! The horses must be made ready! And provisions for the journey! No more delay!

A crowd gathered to stare at the ranting, disheveled newcomer. Some in the crowd pointed and laughed, while others egged him on: Oh great and mighty King of Israel, don't forget to ask for a suitably royal cushion in your chariot—must not let the royal person be dirtied! Remember to add another princess to your collection—we have a few good ones here!

The priest continued to ignore it all, although he picked up his pace. Dirt-covered arms grabbed and poked King

Solomon, slowing him down to the point that he lost the priest. Cursing the crowd, he threatened to have them flogged for their insolence. Wild laughter erupted in response.

A small group of armed guards pushed their way through the crowd. Solomon beamed: Are you here to escort me to a chariot? To take me home to Jerusalem? There will be a fitting reward for your gracious aid.

The guards' captain, stinking of garlic, turned his irritated eyes to the filthy, screaming man who had intruded on his city's normally placid morning: You mad fool, you are causing a disturbance. Quit it and follow us.

One of the armed men hit Solomon with something sharp, stinging the back of his thigh. The sad, confused king stumbled forward, following the small band of armed guards down one alleyway and then another, until the meandering route faded into a blur of darkish passageways, damp clothes hung out to dry, and cursing neighbors.

The group stopped at a guard tower at the city's edge. Solomon felt himself lifted in the air by many different arms and hands. His mind whirred with images of the tall, stooped man with his long knife. He prayed again to the Holy One, Blessed be He.

And then his body hit the dirt road, with his left side in terrible pain, and blood was streaming down from his scalp into his eyes. In the distance, a band of laughing sentries and guards were walking back into the city. Solomon slowly raised himself up again, and with nowhere else to go, followed the road away from the city's gate and watchtower.

His mind emptied. Although he briefly wondered if he would be set upon by vicious beasts, or by robbers, he was unable to care one way or the other, feeling only a need to stay in motion. The sensation of his feet touching the dusty ground made Solomon feel peaceful, and some part of him was afraid of standing still again. After a while, the city and its gates and towers had faded into a tiny speck on the horizon behind him.

It was night. His head pounded from hunger and thirst, and his limbs had grown sore, but he continued to move forward on the road. From the distance, there was now the sound of sweetly melancholy music. As he walked further, he could discern a sad, wistful love song—the young girl singing had kissed her love goodbye, but he never came back for her from his voyage across the sea. She had lived out her days in longing and solitude, staying unmarried, so she could wed her beloved when he finally came home, should he ever come home.

Moved by the song, he veered from the main road to walk in the direction of the music until he reached a merrily lit villa in the otherwise empty, rocky wilderness. In addition to the sweet song, there were happily chattering voices inside. In the light of the torches on the white marble veranda, Solomon saw two large, dark wooden doors with golden handles, which opened easily at his touch.

The interior was a spacious banquet hall with chandeliers, which cast off a festive white light. Spread amongst and between the crowds of elegant, perfumed youths and ladies reclining on couches were low, rectangular black tables covered with cups, pitchers, and plates of food—figs, dates, almonds, small cakes, grilled and spiced meats. Solomon felt his hunger pains acutely.

The walls were decorated with brightly painted murals. In one, mermaids with long flowing hair circled a ship as the sailors looked down upon them, spellbound and ready to jump to their doom. On the opposite wall was a painting of several sphinxes picking greedily at the carcass of a dead king.

Solomon felt a tap on his shoulder.

King Solomon, we have been expecting you tonight. I heard you were nearby, and I was so hoping you would join us. This is my villa, and this is my party. And I am honored to have such a noble guest.

The speaker was a graceful, oval-faced, middle-aged woman with pale skin and long red curls falling neatly over her shoulders. She leaned in and touched his arm.

You are tired from the journey. It has not been an easy time for you, I can tell. But please, come in and rest and eat and enjoy. I want to see you relaxed and smiling.

Solomon forced a smile, thanked her for her hospitality, and apologized for his appearance.

Nonsense, no need to apologize. But first things first. Before you enter my party you need to taste my special honey, and tell me what you think. I keep bees—a hobby—and make my own honey. Here, try some.

The hostess rummaged in a side pocket of her dress, from which she pulled out a small green jar and a spoon. Scooping up a clump of raw, congealed honey, she put the spoon directly into Solomon's mouth. The honey tasted of lavender, and he swooned.

Good. I will give you some before you go, with a spoon. It will lighten and sweeten your wandering. But now come this way.

The charming woman led Solomon through a maze of couches and revelers, none of whom paid him any attention. Even though they were speaking loudly, he could not make out anything they said. There was just a feeling in his body of bliss and soft, undulating motion.

She eventually sat Solomon at an empty couch in the corner, right beneath one of the sphinxes on that wall's mural. The hostess apologized for the less than ideal seat—he was far from the singer and her band. Although weren't they lovely tonight? But he did show up a bit on the later end, he had to admit that, so many better-placed couches had already been taken. Anyway, sit down, she said, and relax and eat. I am sure the rest of your party will be here shortly.

And the woman disappeared back into the crowd.

Solomon was not sure who his party was, but he did not dwell on this detail. His greedy, grasping fingers scooped up figs, dates, apricots, cheese, warm pastries and breads—he could not get enough, and, fortunately, the platter somehow never seemed to empty no matter how much he took. The good food restored Solomon's strength, and he began to feel optimistic again. Perhaps he would soon find his way back to Jerusalem, dispatch Ashmedai back to his demon lair, and put his kingdom in order. He would end the levy of forced labor and declare a holiday festival in which he would distribute free grain and honey to the masses in Jerusalem.

Distracted by the rich food and triumphant daydreams, Solomon gave a start when he finally noticed that two more guests had sat down across from him. They were clearly lovers, a young man and a young woman holding hands tightly and sitting closely pressed to one another. The king of

Israel thought he knew them, but he could not place them exactly—too many people passed through Jerusalem's palace receptions and banquets, and their faces often blurred in his memory. The young man was quite handsome: tall, muscular, with beautiful black hair falling below his shoulders. The woman was equally striking in her dark-haired, dark-eyed beauty. Both were dressed in expensive robes and jewels, with the only mar on their dazzling appearances being identical narrow scars in a crisscross pattern about the middle of their necks, as if their heads had been sewn onto their bodies.

The young man poured three cups of mead, which he assured Solomon was made from the hostess's own exquisite honey. Handing one cup to the king of Israel and one cup to the young woman, the young man raised his hand in a toast:

To Koheleth, who once reigned in Jerusalem, but now wanders these roads as a beggar!

While the young lovers drained their cups, Solomon felt frozen in place, confused by the strange toast. The young man continued:

Our guest does not know his other name. You see, Your Majesty, in this company your true name may prompt someone in this room to notice you, and that would not be for the best. It is never good to distract the revelers. You can never tell how your reputation may be weighed by strangers. So we decided to call you Koheleth. You always seemed girlish to me, little brother, so I thought a feminine alias would suit you.

He raised his cup again:

To Koheleth, king in filth and rags! To the vanity of it all! You thought you were something great, the true, special favorite of the Holy One, Blessed be He? He made you from dirt and you will return to dirt. Kings rise and fall, are born and die, and it happens over and over again: The Holy One, Blessed be He, breathes a soul into a pile of damp dirt and the animated, dancing lump of dirt thinks it is as great as a god. But it will die soon enough, after its soul's light shined ever so briefly in the world, and everything it built will go to ruin. Do you think you are the first arrogant king to build a temple to your god, who has so favored you? Of course not. Your temple, like the others, will fall. Another great king will march someday from the east to Jerusalem, and level His dwelling place for sport and torch your royal city. And then he will be conquered in turn. So it goes, round and round, every king thinking he and his special little realm are eternal and invincible. But it is all a futile waste. The truly eternal earth laughs at you and waits for the right time to unleash its hungry worms to gorge on your flesh. There is nothing new under the sun.

You must see the truth of it now, little brother. Drink, eat, enjoy the party here while you can. You will be in filth again soon enough.

The young man grabbed a fistful of figs, dropping three into his mouth, and two into his beloved's mouth. Once she finished chewing and swallowing, he grabbed the back of her head and kissed her passionately. The young man continued:

Beautiful, isn't she? And the obstacles you placed in the way of my marriage to her. You had unfortunately arranged matters so you could not attend our wedding. She was a sight to see then, in her white gown and white veil: She was dark and comely, a beautiful dove captured from the cleft of the rock, a rose of Sharon, a lily of the valley. She touched my cheek, and stroked my hair, and told me I was her lovely gazelle, her powerful and handsome stag. We spoke our vow: I am my beloved's, and my beloved is mine.

Solomon leaned forward. The fog in his mind had cleared, and he grabbed the edge of the table tightly:

Adonijah, is that you? But you are dead. How can this be? And who is she? Why are you here?

Solomon suddenly sat up straight, turning his head around rapidly, as if noticing his surroundings for the first time.

Where is here?

Relax, little brother, here is the villa of a fine caring lady, who has graciously taken you in so you may get some sustenance. Yes, it is me. I am saddened that you do not recognize Abishag—isn't she lovelier now than she was back in Jerusalem? I think it was a delightful idea for our hostess to arrange this reunion. She stitched our heads back to our bodies just for this special occasion. And as I told you: It is all vain, all that striving and plotting and conniving. You lopped off our heads so we would not marry in this world, and so we wed each other in the next world. Abishag is my destined bride, a match struck by the angels in the Heavenly Court when our souls were released from the treasury of souls in Paradise and sent to earth to enter our mothers' wombs. All you did was make the inevitable unnecessarily difficult.

And for what? So you could sit briefly on your throne and toss up some buildings for the next king to knock down? It is all a waste. Nothing new under the sun, remember that. Just wait and see, our father's kingdom, which he spent his life building, will crumble into petty, warring little states soon enough, before those maggot-sized principalities are squashed by some great empire or other, which in turn will be squashed by some other empire. It all turns and turns and turns without any end and without any point.

But enough talk. I see the hostess is signaling everyone to be silent—no, not there, to your right, yes, there she is. The show is about to start.

The room abruptly went dark. Solomon's heart raced, as he thought in terror that Adonijah's ghost would reach out in vengeance and strangle him. He wanted to flee, but felt unable to move or speak.

In a far corner a light came on again. Into the lighted crook walked a procession: A bejeweled fat man with a golden crown was seated on a throne carried on wooden beams by four lean, bald men dressed in wrinkled linen robes. Solomon could not understand how they had the strength to carry their obese king.

The four men placed their king down in the middle of the light and bowed so low before him their noses touched the floor. The king belched and scratched himself and barked orders in a language Solomon did not know. All of a sudden, the four men jumped to their feet, and pulling out long knives hidden in their clothes, repeatedly stabbed their fat king's belly.

Everything went black.

Solomon had no idea how long he had slept, but when he opened his eyes he was almost blinded by the harsh sun. There was a violent pounding in his head, and his back hurt. He was lying in a spacious villa, but it was a ruin: There were no couches or chandeliers, and the wall murals were faded and stained. The walls and ceiling were pockmarked with gaping holes, and the floor was a mess of broken stones, clay shards, and dry brown weeds. The house appeared to have been abandoned long ago. There was no one else there.

In a corner he saw two skeletons holding hands. They each had, somehow, long thick black human hair still attached to their skulls. Feeling as if their empty eye sockets were watching him, Solomon made for the rotting, broken wooden door.

When he reached the bottom of the steps descending from the veranda he noticed a green satchel packed with little green jars and a handful of spoons, each exactly like the green jar of honey and spoon he recalled from the previous night. Rummaging in the bag, he found a perfumed square of papyrus paper, on which the following was written in neat, large Hebrew letters:

To His Majesty, King Solomon:

It was a great honor to have hosted you as my esteemed and illustrious guest last night. I have left you provisions for your journey. This satchel will supply all of your needs for food and drink. I am truly sorry I did not have more time to speak to you at the party, but so many guests and only one hostess. To return to Jerusalem, walk straight until you reach the main road, and then follow the sun to go west. It is a long walk, but you will reach home in good time.

Best wishes,

L.

Solomon put the satchel on his shoulder and, with no better counsel at hand, he followed the advice in the note, soon locating both the wide, well-trodden road and his bearings heading west. He soon lost track of time in his wanderings. Shunning other travelers, and avoiding cities and settlements, he slept by the side of the road, using his satchel as a pillow. The satchel provided him with a miraculously never-ending supply of lavender honey and mead, which, to his surprise, always satisfied his appetite.

Solomon's mind gradually emptied. He went days without having much of a thought, and even then reflected mostly upon the changing trees or birds. The occasional snarling, vicious beast did not scare him, and in the end, the beast would always ignore him. He sometimes even forgot why he was trying to return to Jerusalem, as he no longer felt much of a desire to be king: It all seemed so vain and pointless. Only the birds' song and the sweet honey and the burning sun seemed real and substantial.

Solomon's hair and beard grew long, knotted, and tangled, as he did not bother to wash himself anymore. The sweet diet took its toll, and his teeth throbbed in pain until he tore them out, rotting tooth by rotting tooth, with his bare hands, leaving his mouth a set of empty gums. He took his simple pleasures—sweet honey and mead, cool early morning air, and shady groves—and waited for his inevitable death, when he would return to the dirt from whence he came.

VI. The Wisdom of Ecclesiastes

ONE EVENING SOLOMON awoke with an unexpected compulsion to stretch his limbs, and started down the road with an unusual briskness. In the distance arose the faint outline of a walled city and a closed gate. An elegantly dressed, but unaccompanied, man walking in the opposite direction approached and addressed the filthy toothless beggar:

Your Majesty, King Solomon, I am delighted to see you have finally returned home. I have been expecting you for some time.

He thought he must have finally succumbed to madness: There was his own body standing in front of him, not as he was now but as he used to be—with silk robes, well-groomed perfumed hair, and adorned with his personal royal signet ring. Although he had many questions, he had lost the habit of speech, and, moreover, it was not easy to speak without any teeth.

I see, Your Majesty, this must all be a bit of a shock. I have been caretaker of your throne ever since you gave me your signet ring. I had to assume your shape and likeness to deflect any uncomfortable questions about my right to be your regent, until Your Majesty had completed his journey. You do recall giving me the ring, with the royal seal?

Solomon remembered and nodded. So this is Ashmedai, lord of the demons, who has been created in my image, he thought.

Well, now that you have returned, it is time to clean you up, Your Majesty. I see you enjoyed the sweet honey of my wife Lilith, perhaps too indulgently, although who could blame you—there really is nothing so wondrously sweet. Come here, do not shy away.

Ashmedai grabbed him by the temples, squeezed hard, and stared into his eyes. Solomon tried to break free, but was too weak. In the beginning there was a terrible pain from the pressure on his skull, but before long the pain migrated to his jaw, as his teeth grew back at a breakneck pace, violently tearing through his gums. Only Ashmedai's rigid grip kept Solomon from staggering to the ground in agony.

He next felt his hair and beard straighten, as if ruthlessly combed and brushed by an invisible, cruel hand. Once untangled, his hair and beard shrank to a more normal length and were sculpted in an elegant style. His robes became silk, and the light scent of rosewater wafted from his chest and hair.

Now that is an improvement, Your Majesty. Much better. You look like yourself—that is to say, like me—again. The messengers of the Throne of Glory, to which I too must submit, have informed me that my time in your palace in Jerusalem has come to an end. The Holy One, Blessed be He, feels that He has now truly answered your many prayers beseeching Him for wisdom.

The signet ring flew into the air and landed on Solomon's ring finger. Ashmedai, the moon, the road, the distant visage of Jerusalem's walls, even the green bag and its honey jars, all instantly vanished. Solomon found himself in his own bed, in his own palace, lying beneath thick blankets. The sleek softness of the old luxurious bedding gently cradled his worn, sore body in a long, dreamless rest.

When he woke, it all felt unreal—Ashmedai, the night with Adonijah and Abishag, the wandering and the honey, and the despair. He summoned a nearby servant to bring him a breakfast of freshly cooked eggs and roasted goat meat, covered in a berry sauce. Food, real, substantial food, had never tasted so magnificent.

With his gullet stuffed, Solomon ambled carelessly to the window. Outside was the panorama of his Jerusalem: People and animals jostling in narrow streets, their shouts and grunts and groans floating up into the air, the sleek palaces of Solomon's wives with tightly closed shutters, which emitted a slight trail of incense smoke, and, above them all, Solomon's great monument, the Temple for the Holy One, Blessed be He, His dwelling place in His sacred, promised land.

But then an image came to the king's mind, of Jerusalem in the generations before King David's conquest. In this daydream, the buildings and streets were different. There were temples to different gods, and even the harsh guttural curses were in another language. They had been sure their world was unshakeable, a fixed point in the universe, until the rampaging King David and his army smashed the old walls and wrecked their city and drove out its people. Nobody knew their names any longer, or recalled their kings and gods. They had been ground back into dust, and remembered and honored no better than stray specks of dirt in the road.

And someday my Jerusalem will be dust, too, Solomon thought: A king will storm in from the East, with hordes of troops, and smash my Temple to the ground. And my wives, with their bitter intrigues and resentments and secret shrines, will all die and be forgotten. The kingdom will fall, maybe even from the inside—some rebellious northern tribal leader will eventually get the better of my royal troops.

The cycle endlessly recurs: Vain, prancing men arise from dust, believe their works to be immortal, but they and their cities and temples are all eventually ground back into the dust from which they came. There is nothing new under the sun.

Solomon saw so clearly now that his life had been spent chasing absurd vanities. His ambition had driven him to erect his great Temple, to wed and possess beautiful queens; he had even tried to outwit the Angel of Death. And to what end? So that he could crumble back into dust to be dinner one evening for a pack of worms, which would look up from heartily nibbling his corpse to watch the next vain conqueror raze Solomon's kingdom.

A laugh erupted from within his chest, shaking his body merrily. So this is Ashmedai's teaching, he mused. I was a glorious king, and then a beggar, and now a king again, and I will end as food for worms. But if this is all so much vanity, why keep striving? Why not renounce the throne and while away the time with sweet wine under the shade of a tree?

Yet he knew this could never be: His mere existence would be a threat to the new king, as Adonijah's life had been a threat to him once, and he would be cut down by his successor, whoever that may be. To enjoy life's fleeting pleasures, the king needed to keep himself alive—and that meant staying on the throne. He was his own prisoner, even though he knew that in a few brief decades—if not sooner—he would lay just as dead as the meanest beggar. Only the earth itself endures, which spit forth humanity from its dust only to pull it back down again into the ground.

King Solomon walked away from the window to sit at the desk near his bed. Reaching for a piece of mostly clean papyrus, he breathed deeply, dipped the stylus into the ink, and began to transcribe in a fever rush all the wisdom that had been vouchsafed for him to learn.

Thus did Israel receive the gift of the Book of Ecclesiastes, may it be a comfort for all in need of the renowned wisdom of King Solomon, who once reigned supreme in Jerusalem.

www.ingramcontent.com/pod-product-compliance
Lightning Source LLC
Chambersburg PA
CBHW032021180726
48283CB00008B/2787

* 9 7 8 1 9 4 5 3 3 0 4 0 7 *